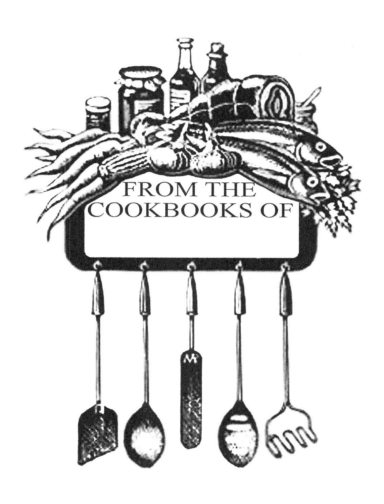

FROM THE
COOKBOOKS OF

Book #2 of the Retro Cookbooks Series

Spotted Dick

and

Other Authentic Dishes with Curious Names

Farrah Knight

Edited by C. Egan

LEAVES OF GOLD PRESS

First published 2012 by Leaves of Gold Press
ABN 67 099 575 078
PO Box 9113
Brighton, 3186
Victoria, Australia

National Library of Australia Cataloguing-in-Publication entry
Author: Knight, Farrah.
Title: Spotted dick : and other authentic dishes with curious names
by Farrah Knight ; edited by C. Egan.
ISBN: 9780987500120 (pbk.)
Series: Retro cookbooks series ; 2.
Notes: Includes bibliographical references and index.
Subjects: Cooking.
Other Authors/Contributors: Egan, C.
Dewey Number: 641.5

CONTENTS

Cover design by
Trish Hart

www.trishhart.com

FOREWORD

Over the years, recipes evolve for one reason or another, and sometimes these reasons give their names to a particular dish, such as 'Half-pay Pudding' - created by a thrifty cook during hard times. On the other hand, some old-fashioned favourites, like 'Zeppelins in a Cloud' derive their titles from the way they look.

The origins of many names are now lost to us, but the names themselves persist in vintage recipe collections handed down to us from past generations.

In the 21st century new and inventive names have arisen, such as 'If Leeks Could Kill...' for a leek and mushroom pie, 'A Fare to Remember' for a beef and cabbage stir fry, 'Remains to Be Seen' for leftover chicken, 'Fauxscargot' for shiitake mushrooms cooked like snails, and 'Quiche and Tell'. Intriguing though these names are, we have decided to list only those that have stood the test of time.

These authentic recipes are presented here almost exactly as they first appeared. In these pages you will find a mixture of weights and measures, temperatures and dimensions, from avoirdupois and imperial to the metric system. To help readers, we have included a page of common conversions at the back of the book.

Toad-in-the Hole, Pigs in Blankets, Gooseberry Fool, Moonshine Pudding, Cock a Leekie Soup, Meat in Ambush, Tuesday Soup, Angels on Horseback, Hedgehog, Black Bottom Pudding... these wacky names are a lot of fun and could provide a talking point at your next dinner-party!

Here they are together, in a collection entitled:

Spotted Dick
and Other Authentic Dishes with Curious Names

1

ANGELS

Angel Cake

Whites of 8 eggs
3/4 cup flour
1 teaspoon cream of tartar
1/4 teaspoon salt
1 cup sugar
3/4 teaspoon vanilla

Beat whites of eggs until frothy; add cream of tartar, and continue beating until eggs are stiff; then add sugar gradually. Fold in flour mixed with salt and sifted four times, and add vanilla. Bake forty-five to fifty minutes in an unbuttered angel-cake pan. After cake has risen and begins to brown, cover with a buttered paper.

SOURCE: FARMER 1918

Angel Food Cake

3/4 cup plain flour
3 tablespoons wheat cornflour (cornstarch)
3/4 cup sugar
2 tablespoons sugar
12 large egg whites at room temperature
1 1/2 teaspoons cream of tartar
1/4 teaspoon salt
3/4 cup sugar
1 1/2 teaspoons vanilla essence
1/2 teaspoon almond essence

Pre-heat oven to 375°.
One by one, in a glass container, separate the egg yolks from the whites. Make sure not a single drop of yolk gets into the egg white. If the white is yolk-free, pour it from the glass container into a bowl.
Sift the cake flour and 3/4 cup plus 2 Tbsp sugar; set aside.
Combine the vanilla and almond essences in a small bowl; set aside. Beat egg whites, cream of tartar and salt until the mixture forms peaks.
Slowly add the other 3/4 cup of sugar, then beat at high speed until stiff peaks form.
Turn your mixer down to low speed and slowly add flour mixture and extracts. Ensure that you fold in the sides and bottom of the mixture in the bowl. Spoon into an ungreased two-piece angel food cake pan.
Swish a knife through the cake mixture to get rid of any air pockets. Bake 30-35 minutes or until top of cake springs back when lightly touched.
Invert pan onto a metal funnel and allow it to cool completely.
To remove the cake from your pan, slide a knife around the sides

of the cake pan to free the crust from the upper rim. Then firmly pat the pan's sides. Try not to use a knife to free the sides of the cake, because this sometimes causes damages.

Turn the cake out upside down onto your serving dish, then take the knife to the new top (which was the bottom) of your pan and carefully cut the cake away from the pan insert.

It is not necessary to cut around the central tube because you merely give the cake a gentle but firm tap or downward shake and it will drop onto the dish.

Cover cake with vanilla icing and decorate with fresh strawberry halves.

SOURCE: ANON

About Angel Food Cake Pans

Angel food cake is usually baked in a tube pan; a tall, round pan with a tube up the center that leaves a hole in the middle of the cake. A bundt pan may also be used, but the fluted sides can make releasing the cake more difficult. The centre tube allows the cake batter to rise higher by 'clinging' to all sides of the pan.

The angel food cake pan should not be greased, unlike pans used to prepare other cakes, this allows the cake to have a surface upon which to crawl up helping it to rise.

After baking, the cake pan is inverted while cooling to prevent the cake from falling in on itself.

Angel food cake is sometimes frosted but more often has some sort of sauce, such as a sweet fruit sauce, drizzled over it. A simple glaze is also popular. Recently, many chefs have popularized the idea of adding aromatic spices such as mace and cloves to the cake.

SOURCE: WIKIPEDIA

Delmonico Ice Cream with Angel Food

Delmonico Ice Cream
2 cups milk
1/8 teaspoon salt
3/4 cup sugar
2 1/2 cups thin cream
Yolks 7 eggs
1 tablespoon vanilla
1 teaspoon lemon

Make custard of milk, sugar, eggs, and salt; cool, strain, and flavor; whip cream, remove whip; there should be two quarts; add to custard, and freeze. Serve plain or with Angel Food.

Angel Food
Whites 3 eggs
1 quart cream whip
1/2 cup powdered sugar
1 1/2 teaspoons vanilla

Beat eggs until stiff, fold in sugar, cream whip, and flavoring; line a mould with Delmonico Ice Cream, fill with the mixture, cover, pack in salt and ice, and let stand two hours.

SOURCE: FARMER, 1918

Angel Hair

Capellini (literally 'thin hair')is a very thin variety of Italian pasta. Like spaghetti, it is rod-shaped, in the form of long strands. Capelli d'angelo (literally 'angel hair')is an even thinner variant of capellini.

Hanks of capellini d'angelo are often sold twisted in a nest-like shape. As a very light pasta, it goes well in soups or with a seafood sauce or other light sauces such as pesto, tomato or garlic sauce. (Wikipedia)

Angel hair cooks quickly. If overcooked it becomes a sticky mess. Use plenty of water to boil this pasta so that it has room to move in the pot.

Before cooking the angel hair, add salt to the boiling water and a few drops of olive oil to stop the pasta threads from sticking together. Add the pasta and stir a few times while it cooks.

After 3 to 5 minutes remove one thread of pasta out of the water with a fork. Rinse with cold water, then take a bite. If the pasta is tender but still firm, it is cooked. If it is still crunchy, cook it for another minute.

When cooked, drain in a colander and add it to your sauce.

SOURCE: ANON

Angel's Food

Take two and a half gills of flour, three and three-quarters gills of sugar, whites of eleven eggs, one teaspoonful of vanilla.

Sift the flour before you measure it ; after measuring it, sift four times; then put one teaspoonful of cream of tartar in the flour, and sift again.

Beat the whites of the eggs to a stiff froth, then stir in the sugar, then the flour, and then the flavour.

Bake in a pan, not greased, forty minutes. When done, turn the pan upside down until perfectly cold. Ice it all over.

SOURCE: HOWSON, 1881

Angels on Horseback

Oysters
Black pepper
Lemon juice
1/2 bacon rasher per oyster
salt
Toothpicks or skewers

Sprinkle oysters with lemon juice, salt and pepper. Wrap each oyster in bacon and secure with toothpick. Place under hot griller, in frying pan or in hot oven, cook quickly until bacon is lightly browned. Serve immediately.

Notes: Sometimes scallops are used in place of oysters. The dish is often served on toast, though if prepared on skewers and grilled, it can be eaten straight from the skewer. A dash of red chili sauce can be added to give a spicy heat.

SOURCE: ANON

About Angels on Horseback

Though the dish is English in origin, the name most likely derives from the French *anges à cheval*; its first occurrence, confirmed by the Oxford English Dictionary and other sources, is in 1888, in Mrs Beeton's Book of Household Management.

However, it must be noted that there is a reference in a New Zealand newspaper to the dish, which includes a brief recipe, from 1882. There appears to be no significance in the connections between oyster/angel and bacon/horse.

SOURCE: WIKIPEDIA

Mock Angel Cake

1 cup sugar
1/3 teaspoon salt
1 1/3 cups flour
2/3 cup scalded milk
3 teaspoons baking powder
1 teaspoon vanilla
Whites 2 eggs

Mix and sift first four ingredients four times. Pour on gradually the scalded milk. Fold in whites of eggs beaten until stiff, and add vanilla.

Turn into an unbuttered angel cake pan and bake in a moderate oven forty-five minutes. This is better for being kept twenty-four hours.

SOURCE: FARMER, 1921

White Mountain Angel Cake

1 1/2 cups egg whites
1 cup bread flour
1 1/2 cups sugar
1/4 teaspoon salt
1 teaspoon cream-of-tartar
1 teaspoon vanilla

Beat egg whites until stiff, using large egg beater. Remove egg beater and add sugar mixed with cream-of-tartar, gradually, folding in with wooden cake spoon.

Cut and fold in flour, mixed with salt, and add flavouring.

Turn into an unbuttered angel cake pan, cover and bake in a moderate oven twenty minutes. Remove cover and bake from twenty to twenty-five minutes.

Invert pan on wire cake cooler and let stand, when cake should, by its own weight, drop from pan.

SOURCE: FARMER, 1921

2
ANIMALS

Armadillo Balls (spicy appetisers)

5 cups cornbread (see recipe below)
1/4 cup butter
1/2 cup chopped celery
1/2 cup chopped onions
1/2 cup chopped green capsicums or chives
2 x 400 g cans chicken broth
1 teaspoon sage
1 x 280 g can cream of chicken soup
2 finely diced chillies
Black pepper
Cayenne pepper
5 eggs, beaten
Flour for coating the Armadillo Balls
Breadcrumbs (also for coating)
Oil for deep frying

Make corn bread (see opposite), allow it to cool and crumble it into small bits.

In a deep saucepan, sauté vegetables in butter. Add crumbled cornbread and chicken broth, and stir until smooth. Add sage and cream of chicken soup. Mix thoroughly.

Add freshly ground black pepper, diced chillies and enough cayenne pepper to suit your preference.

Bake at 180 Celsius until it thickens a little and turns brown. You can stir it during cooking if you wish. Meanwhile heat your deep-frying oil.

When corn-pepper mixture is brown, remove it from the oven and allow it to cool. Place beaten eggs, flour and bread crumbs in 3 separate bowls. Once the corn-pepper mixture is cool, lift out a spoonful and shape it into a ball.

Roll the ball in the flour, then in the beaten egg, then in the bread crumbs. Deep fry on 180 degrees for 2 to 3 minutes - just long enough to give the balls a crisp, crunchy coating.

Cornbread

Half a cup wheat flour
Half a cup yellow corn flour
2 tsp soda
1 tsp salt
3 heaped tbsp sugar
2 cups sour milk or buttermilk
2 tbsp melted cooking fat (eg butter or margarine)

Sift dry ingredients together, add milk and beat well. (If you wish you can add 1/2 cup of grated tasty cheese.)
Coat the insides of two large loaf pans with melted cooking fat. Sprinkle flour in the pans, pour in the batter in equal parts and allow to stand 15 - 20 minutes Bake for 1/2 hour

SOURCE: ANON

Black Cow

2 scoops vanilla ice cream
300 ml Sarsaparilla, Coca Cola or similar sweet, fizzy soft drink
1 tbsp chocolate syrup
50 ml whipped cream
Maraschino cherries

Place ice cream and chocolate syrup in a tall drinking glass. Fill the glass with soft drink. Garnish with whipped cream and top with a maraschino cherry. Serve with a straw and a long spoon.

SOURCE: ANON

Butterfly Cake

2 medium eggs
110g / 4oz self-raising flour
½ teaspoon baking powder
110g / 4oz butter, softened
110g / 4oz sugar

Icing
170g / 6oz icing sugar
85g / 3oz butter, softened
3 drops of vanilla extract
1 tablespoon of milk

12 paper cupcake cases

Preheat the oven to 170 C / 325 F
Pour all the ingredients for the cakes (not the icing ingredients) into a bowl and mix well. Use a spoon to fill each paper cupcake case about half to two thirds full with cake mixture.
Place the filled cases on a baking tray. A flat tray is all right but a muffin tray with indentations to hold the shape of the paper cups is preferable. Put the baking tray in the middle of the pre-heated oven and bake for 30 minutes.

Do not open the oven door for at least 20 minutes, or the cakes might collapse. Cakes are baked when tops are golden brown.
Remove cakes from oven and allow to cool.

Meanwhile, make the icing. Place all the ingredients for the butter icing in a large bowl and stir for about five minutes until all the ingredients are well combined.

To assemble the butterfly, take a sharp knife and slice off the top of each cake. Cut the sliced off 'lid' in half. The halves will be used to form the wings of the butterfly.
Place about a teaspoon full of icing on top of each cake. Then push the "wings" on an angle into the butter icing.
Decorate the cake, if you wish, with sprinkles.

About Butterfly Cake

A butterfly cake is a variant of cupcake,also called fairy cake for its fairy-like "wings". They can be made from any flavour of cake. The top of the fairy cake is cut off or carved out with a spoon, and cut in half. Then, butter cream, whipped cream or other sweet filling (e.g. jam) is spread into the hole. Finally, the two cut halves are stuck into the butter cream to look like butterfly wings. The wings of the cake are often decorated using icing to form various patterns.

SOURCE: WIKIPEDIA

Canary Pudding

2 ozs. of butter
4 ozs. of sugar
6 ozs. of flour
1 small teaspoonful of baking powder
The grated rind of one lemon
1 teaspoonful of essence of lemon
2 eggs
1/2 gill (1/8 pint) of milk.

Beat the butter and sugar to a cream, add the well beaten eggs, then the milk and essence, and, lastly, the flour, baking powder and lemon rind.

Mix well, pour into a well greased mould, and steam for 1 1/2 hours. Serve with lemon sauce.

SOURCE: QUEANBEYAN AGE AND QUEANBEYAN OB-SERVER, 1919

Cats' Tongues (Langues de Chat)
These small cookies date from the 17th century!

60 g softened butter
100 g icing sugar
½ teaspoon vanilla essence
2 egg whites
100 g sifted plain flour

Pre-heat oven to 220°C . In a mixing bowl, cream the butter. Then add the icing sugar and beat the mixture well.

Add the vanilla essence, then gradually add the egg whites, and some of the flour if needed.

Using a metal spoon carefully fold in the rest of flour using a light, swirling action so as not squash out the air bubbles.

Fit the tube to your piping bag and pour the mixture into the bag. Pipe thin tongue-like of dough 7cm long on to ungreased baking trays. Put trays into the preheated oven and bake for about 8 minutes.

While they are baking, rub oil on a rolling pin. This will be the mould for shaping the biscuits.

Remove biscuits from the baking sheet as soon as they are cooked and wrap each one around the rolling pin, so that when they cool they keep a curved shape.

Let them cool on the rolling pin and, when cold, transfer them to a wire rack.

Cats' Tongues do not freeze well but they will keep for up to five days in an airtight container.

SOURCE: ANON

English Monkey

1 cup stale bread crumbs
1/2 cup soft mild cheese, cut in small pieces
1 cup milk
1 tablespoon butter
1 egg
1/2 teaspoon salt
Few grains cayenne

Soak bread crumbs fifteen minutes in milk. Melt butter, add cheese, and when cheese has melted, add soaked crumbs, egg slightly beaten, and seasonings. Cook three minutes, and pour over toasted crackers which have been spread sparingly with butter.

SOURCE: FARMER, 1918

Notes: This recipe might have been invented by the Welsh in response to the dish 'Welsh Rabbit' (an ethnic slur on the poverty and thrift of the Welsh), or by the Scots as a similar reply to 'Scotch Woodcock'.

English Monkey II - Welsh-American

1 tablespoon butter
1 cup bread crumbs
1/2 pound cheese, diced
1 cup whole milk
2 eggs, beaten
Saltine crackers

Break eggs into a cup. Melt butter in saucepan, add bread crumbs and brown them in the butter.

Add cheese and when it is melted, add milk. Stir over medium heat until it thickens and comes to a boil.

Pour in the eggs, stir and remove from fire.

Add salt to taste Serve on salted crackers.

SOURCE: CHICAGO 1930

English Monkey III

1 cup milk,
3/4 cup stale wholewheat bread-crumbs,
3/4 cup shredded tasty cheese
1/2 small onion,
1/2 teaspoon salt,
1/4 teaspoon cayenne,
1 teaspoon dry mustard,
1 teaspoon Worcestershire sauce
1 egg,
2 tablespoons finely chopped parsley,
1 tablespoon finely diced gherkin,
4 slices toast.

Dice the onion finely and fry with one teaspoon of butter in a saucepan. Blend the cheese with two table spoons of milk and add to the sauce pan.

Add the remainder of the milk. Stir until the sauce thickens. Beat the egg slightly and add with salt, cayenne, mustard and Worcester shire sauce. Cook two minutes over low heat.

Add the breadcrumbs. Stir thoroughly once and cook gently two minutes. Add the finely chopped parsley and diced gherkin. Serve at once on hot buttered toast. Garnish with a sprig of parsley. Serves four.

This dish served hot is delicious for breakfast, and when you add a light beetroot or celery and lettuce salad, or hot grilled tomatoes, it makes a pleasant change on the menu for lunch or dinner too.

SOURCE: NORTHERN TIMES, CARNARVON, WA, 1941

Frog Cake

For Sponge Cake:
1.5 cups cake flour
1 cup cornstarch
12 eggs
1.5 cups superfine sugar
2/3 cup unsalted butter, melted and cooled
2 tsp vanilla extract

For Decoration:
1 1/4 cups raspberry glaze
2 cups vanilla icing
green and pink food coloring
4.5 cups vanilla buttercream icing
2 tbsp black icing or small round black lollies for eyes

To make the cake
Grease a 25cm (10 inch) square pan and line base with baking paper.
Sift flours and 1/4 tsp salt together three times to make them light and airy.

Preheat oven to 180C. Using an electric mixer, beat eggs and sugar in a large bowl on medium-high speed for 6 minutes, or until mixture is thick, pale and tripled in volume.

Gradually sift flour mixture over egg mixture while folding in with a large metal spoon until only just combined. Pour mixture into prepared tin. To level batter, gently spin tin on kitchen table.
Bake for 35 to 45 minutes or until cake has shrunk away from the sides slightly and the top springs back when gently touched.
Remove from oven and allow cake to cool in the tin.

When cool, turn out the cake from its tin. Cut it in half crosswise, forming two layers. Spread the raspberry glaze on the bottom later. Place the two halves back together. Cut the cake into 5cm (2 inch) squares.

To assemble the frogs -
Divide the vanilla icing in half. Add a tiny amount of green food coloring to one batch and a drop or two of pink to the other, dyeing each a pale colour. The icing should be think so that it can be poured. Use warm water to thin it if necessary.
Set the cakes on two wire racks, with an equal number on each rack. Set rimmed baking trays below each rack to catch spillage.

Use a small ice cream scoop to top each cake with a dollop of buttercream icing in a dome shape. Pour the icing over the cakes to coat them entirely, using the pink icing for one set and the green icing for the other set. The icing will drip through the rack into the baking trays below. Collect the dripped icing, set in containers (keeping the colors separate) and cover. Let the cakes set for 30 minutes, then pour a second coat and let set for another 30 minutes.
Heat a knife by dipping it in boiling water, and use it to slice through the icing to shape the frog's mouth. Press the knife slightly up and down to open the mouth, revealing the buttercream. Add tiny dots of black icing or the black lollies for the eyes.

About Frog Cake
The Frog cake is a dessert in the shape of a frog's head, composed of sponge cake and cream covered with fondant. It was created by the Balfours bakery in 1922, and soon became a popular treat in South Australia. Originally frog cakes were available exclusively in green, but later brown and pink were added to the range. Since then other variations have been developed, including seasonal varieties (such as snowmen and Easter "chicks"). The frog cake has been called "uniquely South Australian",[1] and has been employed in promoting the state. In recognition of its cultural significance, in 2001 the frog cake was listed as a South Australian Heritage Icon by the National Trust of South Australia.

SOURCE: WIKIPEDIA

Grasshopper Pie

Pie shell
1 1/4 cups chocolate cookie crumbs
1/4 cup sugar
1/3 cup melted butter

Filling
1 envelope gelatin
1/2 cup sugar
1/8 teaspoon salt
1/2 cup cold water
3 eggs, separated
1/4 cup green creme de menthe
2 tablespoons cognac or creme de cacao
1 cup heavy cream, whipped.

Preheat oven to 450 degrees.
To make the pie shell, mix the chocolate crumbs, sugar and butter. Press the mixture against the bottom and sides of a nine-inch pie plate. Bake five minutes, allow to cool and chill in the freezer.
To make filling, combine in the top of a double boiler the gelatin, salt and half the sugar. Stir in the water and blend in the egg yolks, one at a time. Place the mixture over boiling water, stirring constantly until gelatin is dissolved and mixture thickens slightly, four to five minutes.
Remove the mixture from the heat and stir in the creme de menthe and cognac. Add a drop or two of green food dye if desired. Chill, stirring occasionally, until mixture has a consistency resembling unbeaten egg white.
Beat the egg whites until stiff but not dry, then gradually stir in remaining sugar. Continue beating until whites are very stiff. Gently fold them into the gelatin mixture.
Fold in the whipped cream and turn mixture into chilled pie shell. Chill until firm (3 to 4 hours)and garnish, if desired, with additional whipped cream.

SOURCE: ANON

About Grasshopper Pie

Grasshopper Pie was invented in the late 1950s or early 1960s, when chiffon pies were popular. The "grasshopper" title derives from the well-known creme-de-menthe cocktail, created around the same time.

In Australian newspapers, the earliest mention of real grasshopper pie was in the Healesville and Yarra Glen Guardian in 1902:

> 'GRASSHOPPERS AS FOOD.
>
> 'Grasshopper catching is a profit able business in the Philippines. They sell at eight shillings per bushel, in the larger cities of the islands, where the people do not have a chance to get at the insects in the fields.
>
> The grasshopper is a regular article in the markets for the entire year, as after drying they can, be kept indefinitely. It is in the operation of drying ,that the grasshopper is made eatable. Natives will not eat a green, grass hopper, but they eat dried ones by the pocketful in the street, in company, at entertainments, and by the dishful at the table at their homes.
>
> The "hopper" is first so thoroughly dried in the heat of the sun or in the oven that a nice crisp article of food results. This tastes sweet of itself; something like jumbles. The natives usually sweeten the grasshoppers more by using a sprinkling of brown sugar. Then the confectioners make up grass hopper with sugar, chocolate and coloured candy in such a way that a very nice piece of confectionery is obtained.
>
> The housewife of the Philippines takes considerable delight in placing before you a nice grasshopper pie or cake. Grasshopper pie is a most wonderful dish, as the big hoppers are prepared in such a way that they do not lose their form or any of their parts.
>
> Care is taken to keep the grasshoppers intact, and they are artistically arranged on the top crust, while inside are some of the broken hoppers mixed with special foods. Grasshopper cake has the grasshoppers sprinkled through it, and resembles plum cake.'

Hedgehog - Apple

A dish much patronised by our grandmothers.

Required: Six large baking apples, three ounces of moist sugar, two ounces of sweet almonds, red-currant jelly, the rind of half a lemon, two cloves.

Peel, core, and slice the apples, stew them until they are soft, with the sugar, lemon-rind, cloves, and a little water. Then take out the rind and cloves and rub the apple through a sieve.

Shell the almonds and cut them, lengthways into thick shreds. Arrange the apple-pulp in a pretty dish to look as much the shape of a hedgehog as possible.

Stamp out three round pieces of red-currant jelly about the size of a shilling, arrange these down the middle, then stick the shreds of almonds all over the apples.

SOURCE: THE QUEENSLANDER, 1907

Hedgehog - Chocolate

2½ oz desiccated chocolate
2 oz cornflour
2 oz castor sugar
One pint of milk
A few sweet almonds

Boil half the milk in a clean saucepan. While it is heating -- and mind you do not let it boil over -- put the cornflour into a small basin, and mix it into a smooth paste with the rest of tho milk.

Add the chocolate and sugar by degrees, and be careful that there are no lumps. Take a pint mould--a plain oval one, if you have it -- and fill it with cold water; this you pour away when the mixture is ready.

When the milk boils pour the contents of the basin into the saucepan, and stir briskly over the fire for five or six minutes, or until the mixture thickens.

Do not leave it at this critical point, or it may go into lumps. Pour it into the mould; and, when the shape is turned out, stick almonds, sliced into thin pieces, all over it.

SOURCE: THE QUEENSLANDER, 1903

Hedgehog - Modern

This sweet slice is widely available in cafes and bakeries in Australia.

1/2 cup (125g) butter
1/2 cup (60g) chopped walnuts
150g castor sugar
1/4 cup (45g) glace cherries
2 tablespoons cocoa
1/2 teaspoon vanilla essence
2 tablespoons dessicated coconut
2 cups (220g) crushed sweet biscuits
1 egg, beaten
A greased 20 cm square pan

Melt butter and sugar together, add cocoa and mix well. Remove from heat and stir in coconut and egg. Add walnuts, cherries and vanilla. Stir in biscuit crumbs and mix well.

Press into square pan and chill. Cut into squares. May be iced with chocolate glace icing and sprinkled with coconut, Hundreds and Thousands, or chocolate sprinkles.

Chocolate Glace Icing

1 cup (270g) icing sugar
1 1/2 tablespoons water
2 tablespoons grated chocolate or 1 tbsp cocoa

Sift sugar and put in a saucepan with chocolate or cocoa. Add the water and stir until warm. Pour over the slice and spread evenly.

SOURCE: ANON

Hummingbird Cake

Cake
1 x 450 g can crushed pineapple
1 cup plain flour
½ cup self-raising flour
½ teaspoon bicarbonate of soda
½ teaspoon ground cinnamon
1 cup brown sugar, firmly packed.
½ cup desiccated coconut
1 cup mashed over ripe bananas
2 eggs, lightly beaten
¾ cup vegetable oil

Cream cheese frosting
50 g butter, softened
1 x 250 g cream cheese, softened
2 teaspoons vanilla essence
1 cup icing sugar

Grease a deep 23 cm round cake pan and line base with baking paper.
Drain pineapple in a fine sieve, pressing out as much syrup as possible, reserving ¼ cup syrup. Sift flours, soda and cinnamon in a large bowl. Stir in sugar and coconut. Make a well in the centre.
Add combined bananas, eggs, oil, pineapple and reserved syrup. Mix until combined. Pour mixture into prepared pan.
Cook at 180°C for about 1 hour, or until cooked when tested with skewer. Cover with foil if top is over browning. Stand cake in pan for 5 minutes and turn out onto wire rack to cool.
Cream cheese frosting: Beat butter, cream cheese and essence in a small bowl with electric mixer until light and fluffy.
Gradually beat in icing sugar until smooth. Spread on top and sides of cake

SOURCE: ANON

Monkey Bread

1/2 cup butter
1/2 cup chopped walnuts
1 cup brown sugar
2 tbs. water
3 tbs. cinnamon
560 g plain scone dough (Approx. 4 3/4 cups self raising flour mixed with pure cream to a dough consistency)
rolled out to 2 cm thick)
1/2 cup sultanas (optional)

Preheat oven to 250C.
Sprinkle 3 Tbs. of chopped nuts in bottom of well-greased Bundt
or angel food cake pan. In a saucepan melt butter, add remaining
nuts, brown sugar and water; heat to a boil, stirring constantly.
Put a layer of scone dough ; sprinkle some of the mixture over
the dough, sprinkle with a little cinnamon, keep layering until all
ingredients are used. Bake 20 to 25 minutes.
If using sultanas include them among the layers.

SOURCE: ANON

Notes: Monkey bread, also called sticky bread, African coffee cake,
golden crown, pinch-me cake, bubbleloaf and monkey brains is a
sweet, sticky, gooey pastry served in the United States for breakfast.

SOURCE: WIKIPEDIA

Pigs in Blankets

2 sheets of puff pastry
16 cocktail sausages

Preheat oven to 190 degrees C.
Lightly grease a large baking tray.
Cut the puff pastry sheets into 8 squares.
Wrap each cocktail sausage in a square of dough.
Place on prepared baking tray.
Bake in preheated oven for 15 minutes, until golden
Serve with tomato sauce.

SOURCE: ANON

#

Porcupine - Apple

Make a syrup by boiling one and a half cupfuls of water for
ten minutes.
Wipe, pare, and core eight apples. Put them in the syrup at once,
or they may discolor. Cook until soft, occasionally skimming the
syrup during cooking.
Apples cook better when covered with the syrup, therefore it is
better to use a deep saucepan, and have two cookings.
Drain the apples from the syrup; cool, and fill the centres with
marmalade, preserved ginger, or jelly, and stick the apples with almonds blanched, and split in halves lengthwise.

SOURCE: THE DAILY NEWS, PERTH, WA, 1903

Porcupine Balls

Combine 1 1/2 pounds minced beef with 1/2 cup uncooked rinsed rice., 1 teaspoon salt, 1/4 teaspoon pepper, 1 tablespoon grated onion.

Blend well and shape into meat balls. Mix one tin of condensed tomato soup with an equal quantity of water and heat to the boiling point. Drop meat balls into the boiling soup. Cover and cook over simmer heat for 1 hour.

Serve with fresh buttered spinach or carrots, with apple pie to follow.

SOURCE: TOWNSVILLE DAILY BULLETIN, 1950

Toad in the Hole

1 lb. of tender beef steak,
1/2 an ox kidney,
3 oz. of flour,
2 eggs,
1 pint of milk,
Pepper and salt.

Put the flour into a basin, make a well in the middle, put in eggs and mix gradually, add milk by degrees.

Beat well and add half the pepper and salt; cut steak into pieces the way of the grain, also cut up kidney, put them in a well greased Yorkshire pudding tin, sprinkle with remainder of pepper and salt and pour batter over. Bake one hour.

SOURCE: LIVERPOOL HERALD NSW, 1904

Notes: Instead of pieces of steak and kidney you can use fried fat sausages.

Welsh Rabbit I (Also called 'Welsh Rarebit')

1 tablespoon butter
1/4 teaspoon salt
1 teaspoon corn-starch
1/4 teaspoon mustard
1/2 cup thin cream
Few grains cayenne
1/2 lb. soft mild cheese cut in small pieces
Toast or wafer crackers

Melt butter, add corn-starch, and stir until well mixed, then add cream gradually, while stirring constantly, and cook two minutes. Add cheese, and stir until cheese is melted. Season, and serve on wafer crackers or bread toasted on one side, rarebit being poured over untoasted side. Much of the success of a rarebit depends upon the quality of the cheese. A rarebit should be smooth and of a creamy consistency, never stringy.

SOURCE: FARMER 1918

About Welsh Rabbit

Wikipedia says: 'The name of the dish originates from 18th-century Great Britain. The first recorded use of the term 'Welsh Rabbit' was in 1725, but the origin of the term is unknown. It may be an ironic name coined in the days when the Welsh were notoriously poor; only better-off people could afford butcher's meat, and while in England rabbit was the poor man's meat, in Wales the poor man's meat was cheese. It might also be understood as a slur against the Welsh: if a Welshman went rabbit hunting, this would be his supper.

'Some recipes for Welsh rarebit have become textbook savoury dishes listed by culinary authorities ... who tend to use the form Welsh rarebit, emphasising that it is not a meat dish.

Perhaps authors also used 'rarebit' in an effort to modify the slur on the poverty and thrift of the Welsh.

'The term Welsh rarebit is evidently a later corruption of Welsh rabbit, being first recorded in 1785 by Francis Grose. According to the Oxford English Dictionary, 'Welsh rarebit' is an "etymologizing alteration. There is no evidence of the independent use of rarebit".

'Michael Quinion writes: "Welsh rabbit is basically cheese on toast (the word is not 'rarebit' by the way, that's the result of false etymology; 'rabbit' is here being used in the same way as 'turtle' in 'mock-turtle soup', which has never been near a turtle, or 'duck' in 'Bombay duck', which was actually a dried fish called bummalo)".

'The word rarebit has no other use than in Welsh rabbit and "rarebit" alone has come to be used in place of the original name.

'Various recipes for Welsh rarebit include the addition of ale, mustard, ground cayenne pepper or ground paprika and Worcestershire Sauce. The sauce may also be made by blending cheese and mustard into a Béchamel sauce or Mornay sauce.

'Welsh rarebit blended with tomato (or tomato soup) is known as Blushing Bunny.'

Welsh Rabbit II

1 tablespoon butter
1/4 teaspoon mustard
1/2 lb. soft mild cheese, cut in small pieces
Few grains cayenne
1/3 to 1/2 cup ale or lager beer
1/4 teaspoon salt
1 egg

Put butter in chafing-dish, and when melted, add cheese and sea-sonings; as cheese melts, add ale gradually, while stirring constant-ly; then egg slightly beaten. Serve same as Welsh Rarebit I.

SOURCE: FARMER, 1918

Welsh Rabbit III

40 grams stale bread crusts,
4 tablespoons of milk,
50 grams grated cheese,
1 teaspoon mustard,
1 teaspoon salt,
Pinch of pepper,
15 grams butter,
4 rounds of toast

Soak the stale crusts in water and squeeze them out. Put the soaked crusts into a bowl and add the milk, half the cheese, salt, pepper and mustard. Stir until well mixed. Melt butter in a saucepan then add bread and cheese mixture. Stir well and cook until hot. Spread the mixture on the rounds of toast. Sprinkle the rest of the cheese over the toast and grill until the topping is light brown. Serve hot.

SOURCE: BATHURST

Yorkshire "Moggie"

2 cups plain flour,
¾ cup sugar
3 tablespoonfuls treacle,
2 teaspoonfuls ginger,
1 teaspoonful bicarbonate of soda,
3 oz lard.

Mix dry ingredients together, put in treacle and lard, and melt.
Mix soda in a tablespoonful of milk.
Mix with milk, and bake in a slow oven.

SOURCE: ANON

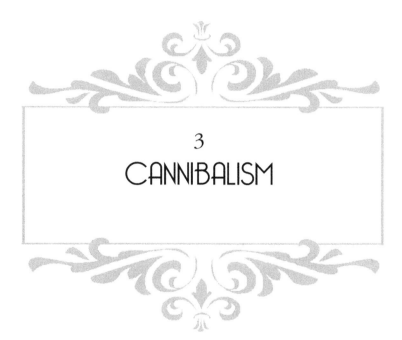

3

CANNIBALISM

Brown Betty

Put a layer of apples, chopped fine, in a baking-dish, sprinkle with cinnamon and sugar, a layer of bread-crumbs with butter, cinnamon and sugar, then another layer of apples, and repeat until the dish is filled.

Bake it an hour to an hour and a half in a good oven. Make a sauce of one pint of milk, one egg, four tablespoonfuls of sugar; let it come to a boil; flavor with vanilla, lemon, nutmeg or wine, as you please.

SOURCE: HOWSON, 1881

About Brown Betty

Brown Betty is a traditional American dessert made from fruit (usually apple, but also berries or pears) and sweetened crumbs. Similar to a cobbler or a bread pudding, it consists of a baked pudding made with layers of sweetened and spiced fruit and buttered bread crumbs.

It is usually served with a lemon sauce or whipped cream.

The dish was first mentioned in print in 1864. A recipe from 1877 uses apple sauce and cracker crumbs.

SOURCE: WIKIPEDIA

Bride Cake

Twelve eggs,
1 1/4 lb. butter,
1 1/4 lb. plain flour,
2 pieces of citron peel,
1 wineglassful each of brandy, sherry and rosewater,
2 1/2 teaspoonfuls baking powder,
1 1/4 lb. brown sugar,
2 lb. seeded raisins,
1 lb. sultanas,
1 1/2 lb. currants,
1/2 lb. of ground almonds,
1 packet mixed spice,
1/2 teaspoonful ground spice,
1 teaspoonful ground cloves,
1 teaspoonful cinnamon.

Prepare the fruit and peel, and rub in as much flour as it will take. Pound the almonds in the rosewater.

Cream the butter and sugar, add the beaten yolks of the eggs, then the fruit flavorings, spice, cloves and cinnamon, whites of eggs whipped stiff, and lastly lap in lightly the remaining flour.

Bake in a moderate oven from 2 to 3 hours; if preferred can be baked in two cake tins. When cold, ice cake and decorate.

SOURCE: SUNDAY TIMES, PERTH 1925

Duchess Soup

4 cups chicken stock
1/3 cup butter
2 slices carrot, cut in cubes
1/4 cup flour
2 slices onion
1 teaspoon salt
2 blades mace
1/8 teaspoon pepper
1/2 cup grated mild cheese
2 cups scalded milk

Cook vegetables three minutes in one and one-half tablespoons butter, then add stock and mace; boil fifteen minutes, strain, and add milk. Thicken with remaining butter and flour cooked together; add salt and pepper. Stir in cheese, and serve as soon as cheese is melted.

SOURCE: FARMER, 1921

Fat Rascals

250 g plain flour
100 g butter, softened
75 g currants
50 g mixed citrus peels
1 1/2 teaspoons baking powder
75 g golden caster sugar
150 ml whipping cream (you can use sour cream or creme fraiche if you wish)
1 egg, beaten
Whole blanched almonds and glace cherries to decorate

Pre-heat the oven to 220C/425F and grease a baking tray or line it with baking paper.

Rub the butter into the flour until it resembles breadcrumbs. Add the remaining dry ingredients and mix well.

Add the cream and mix until it becomes a firm dough. Roll the mixture out on a floured board, to about 2.5cm thickness and stamp out rounds, of about 8cm in diameter.

You can also shape the fat rascals by hand; take a piece of dough about the size of a small egg, and make a small ball, and flatten it out slightly into bread roll shapes.

Arrange these on the greased baking tray and glaze them generously with the beaten egg. Decorate by putting two whole blanched almonds on top, with a halved glace cherry for decoration - pushing them down gently into the dough, so they stick on.

Bake for 15 to 20 minutes, or until the rascals have risen and are golden brown. Allow to cool on a wire cooling rack.

Store them in an airtight tin for up to 4 days.

About Fat Rascals

There are dozens of Fat Rascal recipes throughout Yorkshire. A fat rascal, also called the Yorkshire tea biscuit or turf cake, is a type of cake, similar to the scone in both taste and ingredients. The fat rascal often has no definitive shape and is relatively easy to make. First baked in Elizabethan times and originating in Yorkshire, it is considered a biscuit. Found in bakeries all over Yorkshire, fat rascals are a cross between a scone and a rock cake, but tend to be slightly richer than both.

SOURCE: WIKIPEDIA

BBC Food suggests: 'Serve them warm or cool with a dollop of extra thick double cream.'

Hermits

1/3 cup butter
1/3 cup raisins, stoned and cut in small pieces
2/3 cup sugar
1 egg
1/2 teaspoon cinnamon
2 tablespoons milk
1/4 teaspoon clove
13/4 cups flour
1/4 teaspoon mace
2 teaspoons baking powder
1/4 teaspoon nutmeg

Cream the butter, add sugar gradually, then raisins, egg well beaten, and milk. Mix and sift dry ingredients and add to first mixture. Roll mixture a little thicker than for Vanilla Wafers.

SOURCE: FARMER, 1918

Lady Cake

One cupful of butter, two cupfuls of sugar, three of flour, one of milk, two teaspoonfuls of baking powder, one teaspoonful of almond flavouring, and the whites of eight eggs.
Bake in a square pan.

SOURCE: HOWSON, 1881

Lady Fingers

Whites 3 eggs
1/3 cup flour
1/3 cup powdered sugar
1/8 teaspoon salt
Yolks 2 eggs
1/4 teaspoon vanilla

Beat whites of eggs until stiff and dry, add sugar gradually, and continue beating. Then add yolks of eggs beaten until thick and lemon-colored, and flavoring. Cut and fold in flour mixed and sifted with salt. Shape four and one-half inches long and one inch wide on a tin sheet covered with unbuttered paper, using a pastry bag and tube. Sprinkle with powdered sugar, and bake eight minutes in a moderate oven.
Remove from paper with a knife. Lady Fingers are much used for lining moulds that are to be filled with whipped cream mixtures. They are often served with frozen desserts, and sometimes put together in pairs with a thin coating of whipped cream between, when they are attractive for children's parties.

SOURCE: FARMER, 1918

Lemon Queens

1/4 lb. butter
Yolks 4 eggs
1/2 lb. sugar
5 ozs. flour
Grated rind 1 lemon
1/4 teaspoon salt
3/4 tablespoon lemon juice
1/4 teaspoon soda (scant)
Whites 4 eggs

Cream the butter, add sugar gradually, and continue beating. Then add grated rind, lemon juice, and yolks of eggs beaten until thick and lemon-colored. Mix and sift soda, salt, and flour; add to first mixture and beat thoroughly.
Add whites of eggs beaten stiff. Bake from twenty to twenty-five minutes in small tins.

SOURCE: FARMER, 1918

Lumberjack Cake

Cake
2 large apples, peeled, cored and finely chopped
1 cup chopped dates
1 teaspoon bicarbonate of soda
1 cup boiling water
125 g butter, softened
1 teaspoon vanilla essence
1 cup caster sugar
1 egg
1½ cups plain flour

Topping
60 g butter
½ cup brown sugar
½ cup milk
2/3 cup shredded coconut

Grease and line a deep 23 cm square cake pan.

Combine apples, dates and bicarbonate of soda in a bowl. Add the water and leave for 10 minutes.
Beat butter, sugar, vanilla, and egg until light and fluffy. Add butter to apple mixture and fold in flour.
Pour into prepared pan and bake in moderate oven for 50 minutes.

Topping:
Combine ingredients in a saucepan and stir until butter melts and sugar dissolves.
Remove cake from oven and carefully spoon topping mixture over cake. Return to oven and bake for another 20 minutes.
Stand cake for 5 minutes before turning onto a wire rack.
This cake can also be made without the topping.

SOURCE: ANON

Napoleons

Bake three sheets of pastry, pricking before baking. Put between the sheets Cream Filling. Spread top with Confectioner's Frosting, sprinkle with pistachio nuts blanched and chopped, crease in pieces about two and one-half by four inches, and cut with sharp knife

Cream Filling
7/8 cup sugar
2 eggs
1/3 cup flour
2 cups scalded milk
1/8 teaspoon salt
1 teaspoon vanilla or
1/2 teaspoon lemon extract

Mix dry ingredients, add eggs slightly beaten, and pour on gradually scalded milk. Cook fifteen minutes in double boiler, stirring constantly until thickened, afterwards occasionally. Cool and flavour.

Confectioners' Frosting
2 tablespoons boiling water or cream
Confectioners' sugar
Flavouring

To liquid add enough sifted sugar to make of right consistency to spread; then add flavouring. Fresh fruit juice may be used in place of boiling water. This is a most satisfactory frosting, and is both easily and quickly made.

SOURCE: FARMER, 1918

Nuns

Choux Pastry Profiteroles
1 cup water
120g butter
Pinch of sugar
1 cup sifted plain flour
6 eggs at room temperature
Cooking oil

Cream Filling
3 large egg yolks, plus 2 large egg whites
100g caster sugar
40g cornflour
300ml whole milk
75g plain chocolate, broken

Easy Fondant Icing
300g package pre-made royal icing
50g cooking chocolate

Choux Pastry Profiteroles
Preheat oven to 200°C. Brush two baking trays lightly with oil to grease. Line them with greased baking paper.
Cut the butter into small pieces so it melts quickly and evenly.
Place water and butter in a saucepan over medium heat. Cook, stirring with a wooden spoon, for 3-4 minutes or until butter melts. As soon as the mixture comes to the boil, add all the flour at once. Beat until well combined. Turn down heat to low and cook, stirring, for 1-2 minutes or until the mixture forms a ball and begins to come away from the side of the saucepan.
Set aside for 5 minutes to cool slightly.

Transfer the mixture to the bowl of an electric mixer. Add 5 eggs and continue to mix until completely combined and the batter has a smooth, silky texture. Stop the machine and check the consistency of the batter. It should form a peak with a tip that falls over.

It should just fall from the spoon but still hold its shape.
If it is too stiff, beat in the white of the remaining egg. Check again and, if necessary, add the yolk. Do not over-beat.

Set the mixture aside to cool slightly so the eggs don't cook when they are beaten in. The amount of egg required varies with each batch. It depends how big the eggs are and how much egg the flour absorbs. Too much egg will make the choux rise unevenly and spread. Not enough egg and the choux will be stodgy.
Spoon 25-30 teaspoonsful of the mixture onto tray, about 3cm apart.

Or you can use a pastry bag fitted with a 1.5cm-diameter plain piping nozzle to pipe the mixture into 1-tablespoon mounds onto the baking tray leaving about 2 inches between. Brush the tops with a little of the remaining egg. Bake in preheated oven for 25 minutes or until the profiteroles are puffed and golden.

When you break one open, it should be hollow. Remove from the oven and Use a skewer or a small knife to pierce the base of each profiterole to release the steam. Return the profiteroles to the oven and leave them for 15 minutes to dry out. Remove the profiteroles from the oven and transfer to a wire rack to cool.

Cream Filling

Melt chocolate over simmering water in a double saucepan. Place egg yolks, sugar and cornflour in a bowl and beat until pale and thick. Heat milk in a saucepan until just below boiling point, then gradually pour over the egg yolk mixture, stirring well. Pour the mixture back into a clean saucepan then heat over a low heat, stirring constantly, for about 10 minutes, or until thickened. Do not allow to boil. Remove from the heat, add melted chocolate and stir until smooth. Allow to cool for a few minutes. Beat the egg whites until holding stiff peaks, then fold into the mixture. Leave until completely cold before filling the profiteroles.
Split the cooled profiteroles horizontally and use a teaspoon to fill with cream.

Fondant Icing

Melt the chopped royal icing and broken chocolate together in a double saucepan over simmering water. Stir until smooth. Remove from the heat but keep the bowl over the pan because the icing sets quickly as it cools.

Spoon icing over each filled profiterole, leave to set, and then serve. Keep in refrigerator and consume within 24 hours.

SOURCE: ANON

About Nuns

Nuns (Religieuses) are cream puffs (profiteroles) made of choux pastry, filled with a custard-like pastry cream in assorted flavors - such as coffee, vanilla and chocolate - and topped with dark brown fondant icing.

These delicious French pastries are said to resemble nuns wearing a dark habit. They are made of two choux pastry cases , or profiteroles, a large one on the bottom and a smaller one on top, joined together with buttercream. The pastry is filled with confectioner's custard and iced with a chocolate or coffee topping. Sometimes the baker pipes the buttercream, to resemble delicate ruffles.

Religieuses originated in the mid-nineteenth century, though choux pastry was invented as long ago as 1540

Piccaninnies

Scrub a large potato and bake it in its jacket until soft. Cut in half lengthwise, scoop out the middle and mix with any of the following fillings:

1. Equal quantities of cooked shredded cabbage, diced carrot and turnip bound with white sauce and flavoured with a dash of piquant sauce.

2. Roughly chopped kipper bound with mustard sauce.

3. Shredded winter greens cooked in a very little water with some shreds of bacon, flavoured with salt, pepper and mustard, and bound with enough flour to thicken.

Pile up whichever mixture you choose in one half of the potato jacket, put the other half on top and press together. Replace in the oven to heat through.

SOURCE: MINISTRY OF FOOD, LONDON, 1942

About Piccaninnies

Pickaninny (also picaninny or piccaninny) is a term in English which refers to children of black descent or a racial caricature thereof. It is a pidgin word form, which may be derived from the Portuguese pequenino (an affectionate term derived from pequeno, "little"). In the Creole English of Surinam the word for a child is pikin ningre (literally "small negro"). The term pickaninny has also been used in the past to describe aboriginal Australians. Historically the use of Pickaninny may have been used as a term of affection, but it is now considered a derogatory term.(Wikipedia)

Presumably the dish got its name because the potatoes in their jackets resembled babies wrapped in their swaddling clothes. Since this term passed out of favour, this dish is now called 'baked potatoes'.

Poor Knights of Windsor

8 slices bread 1/2-inch thick A little white wine or milk A little butter and a little jam.

Put white wine or milk and sugar into a dish; dip the bread in it on both sides. Then fry the bread gently, on both sides, in a little hot fat. Dish up on a hot plate and spread jam, sugar or cinnamon over it.

SOURCE: WESTERN MAIL, PERTH, WA, 1931

Sally Lunn I

Take 2 oz. butter, one and a-half gills milk, three-quarter pounds flour, one ounce German yeast, two tablespoonfuls sugar, and egg, and a good pinch of salt.

Put butter into a saucepan, and allow it to melt. When melted, add to it one and a half gills of milk.

Put the yeast into a basin with the salt, and work it with a wooden spoon. Then pour on milk and butter, which which should be just tepid.

Beat the egg until it is frothy, add it to the milk, and pour these among the flour : mix all-well together.

For this quantity grease two tins, fill each tin three parts, and stand in warm place to rise for about half-an-hour.

Then place in a quick oven, and bake until a pale brown colour.

When cooked, cut in slices and butter them. Put together again and serve.

SOURCE: THE QUEENSLANDER, 1903

Sally Lunn II

Soak a tablespoonful of yeast crumbs in warm water, enough to corn it when soft; beat in flour to make stiff dough ; set to raise; when thoroughly up take an egg, half cup sugar, tablespoonful of butter, one coffee cup warm milk, one pint flour, put in flour, beat all well, set to rise in crock or bowl ; when up beat down good, put in pan, bake in moderate 'oven. Is nice for tea.

SOURCE: THE NORTH EASTERN ENSIGN, BENALLA, VIC. 1886

About Sally Lunn

Sally Lunn - originally called Solange Luyon - was a young Huguenot refugee who sailed from France to England in 1680. She started a bakery in to city of Bath. Her signature product was a delicious round brioche-type loaf now known as the Sally Lunn Bun.

The bun's fame spread throughout the world and to this day, versions of the Sally Lunn Bun can be found in Canada, The United States, New Zealand and Australia

4
DEVILS

Devilled Almonds

Blanch the almonds to be devilled by throwing them Into boiling water Let stand for a few minutes. Then remove the brown peel, and wipe the almonds perfectly dry.

Melt in a frying-pan sufficient butter, and add salt and a pinch of cayenne pepper.

When the butter Is boiling, drop the almonds In one by one, and cook for about 20 minutes or until the almonds are nice and crisp. Strain and place on blotting paper.

Sprinkle a very little salt, to which has been added just a suspicion of cayenne pepper. Put them in a tin, cover securely, and they will keep crisp.

SOURCE: TOWNSVILLE DAILY BULLETIN, 1921

Devilled Biscuits

'Many diners of the superior sex - I am not a Suffragette, as will be seen by the supremacy I give to men - relish devilled biscuits.

'Take six water biscuits, dip them in oiled fresh butter, and sprinkle them well with black pepper. Grill them over a clear fire until a light brown colour and crisp, basting them with butter all the time.

'Then pour a little more butter over, and serve very hot. Send some grated Parmesan cheese to table   with the biscuits, or sprinkle a layer of cheese over them.'

SOURCE: EVELYN OBSERVER AND BOURKE EAST RE-CORD, VIC. 1913

Devilled Eggs. I

Cut three hard-boilod eggs in thin slices. Cook in the chafing-dish two tablespoonfuls of butter, a teaspoon of dry mustard, two ta-ble- spoonfuls of tomato catsup, same of Worces- tershire sauce, one of mushroom catsup, two drops of tabasco, and a pinch of salt. When this boils add the sliced eggs, and pour over rounds of buttered toast.

SOURCE: THE SYDNEY MORNING HERALD, 1905

Note: If you want the eggs to look fancier, pack the egg filling into a freezer bag, cut off of one corner of the bag and pipe filling into the egg white halves.

Devilled Eggs. II

Three or four eggs
Anchovy sauce
Some cayenne, mustard and cress.

Boil three or four eggs hard. Cut them in halves when cold, and cut a piece off the end of each to make it stand straight. Mix the yolks with a teaspoonful of anchovy sauce and some cayenne. Fill the whites with the mixture; garnish with mustard and cress, and with any of the filling left over formed into little heaps round the dish.

SOURCE: THE WESTERN CHAMPION AND GENERAL ADVERTISER FOR THE CENTRAL-WESTERN DISTRICTS, 1905

Note: If you want the eggs to look fancier, pack the egg filling into a freezer bag, cut off of one corner of the bag and pipe filling into the egg white halves.

Devilled Muscatels

In addition to serving devilled almonds at your next party, try some devilled muscatels as well. Get the large Italian variety, and pick the fruit off the stems. Heat a little Lucca oil or butter in a pan, and throw the muscatels in. Cook gently for about five minutes, turning over and over all the time. Have a large sheet of brown paper spread out on the table, sprinkled liberally with cayenne pepper, salt and cinnamon, lift the muscatels out with a perforated slicer, and roll in the powdered mixture. Do not bottle until quite cold.

SOURCE: MIRROR, PERTH, WA, 1932

Devilled Oysters

Open five large oysters, do not take them from their shells; under each oyster put salt and cayenne pepper, as much of each as thought necessary. let tho liquor remain in the shell; place each shell containing oyster upon a gridiron with a small knob of butter upon top of each; cook for about four minutes on a nice clear fire. Serve on a serviette, and have some daintily rolled bread and butter on a plate to be partaken of with the oysters.

SOURCE: THE DAILY NEWS, PERTH, WA 1908

Devilled Tomatoes

Peel and slice thickly the required quantity of tomatoes, rub some raw mustard into a little butter, and coat the tomatoes well with this. Then give a liberal dusting of black and coralline pepper, and bake or grill them.

SOURCE: THE QUEENSLANDER, 1904

Devil's Food Cake 1

1/2 cup butter
5 teaspoons baking powder
2 cups sugar
Whites 4 eggs
Yolks 4 eggs
4 squares chocolate
1 cup milk
1/2 teaspoon vanilla
22/3 cups flour
1/2 teaspoon salt

Cream the butter, and slowly add one-half of the sugar. Beat yolks of eggs until thick and lemon-coloured, and slowly add the remaining sugar.

Combine mixtures, and add alternately milk and flour mixed and sifted with baking powder and salt; then add whites of eggs beaten stiff, chocolate melted, and vanilla.

Bake forty-five to fifty minutes in an angel cake pan. Cover with White Mountain Cream (see next page).

White Mountain Cream for Devil's Food Cake 1

1 cup sugar
1 teaspoon vanilla or
1/3 cup cold water
1/2 tablespoon lemon juice
White 1 egg

Put sugar and water in saucepan, and stir to prevent sugar from adhering to saucepan; heat gradually to boiling-point, and boil without stirring until syrup will thread when dropped from tip of spoon or tines of silver fork.

Pour syrup gradually on beaten white of egg, beating mixture constantly, and continue beating until of right consistency to spread; then add flavouring and pour over cake, spreading evenly with back of spoon. Crease as soon as firm.

If not beaten long enough, frosting will run; if beaten too long, it will not be smooth. Frosting beaten too long may be improved by adding a few drops of lemon juice or boiling water.

This frosting is soft inside, and has a glossy surface. If frosting is to be ornamented with nuts or candied cherries, place them on frosting as soon as spread.

SOURCE: FARMER, 1918

Devil's Food Cake II

4 squares unsweetened chocolate
1/2 cup sugar
1/2 cup sugar
1/4 cup sour milk
1/2 cup sweet milk
1 egg
Yolk 1 egg
11/8 cups flour
1/4 cup butter
1/2 teaspoon soda
1/2 teaspoon vanilla

Melt chocolate over hot water, add one-half cup sugar, and gradually sweet milk; then add yolk of egg, and cook until mixture thickens. Set aside to cool.

Cream the butter, add gradually one-half cup sugar, egg well beaten, sour milk, and flour mixed and sifted with soda. Combine mixtures and add vanilla.

Bake in shallow cake pans, and put between and on top boiled frosting. Add to filling one-fourth cup raisins seeded and cut in pieces, if desired.

Ice with Boiled Frosting (see next page)

Boiled Frosting for Devil's Food Cake II

1 cup sugar
1/2 cup water
Whites 2 eggs
1 teaspoon vanilla, or 1/2 tablespoon lemon juice

Put sugar and water in saucepan, and stir to prevent sugar from adhering to saucepan; heat gradually to boiling-point, and boil without stirring until syrup will thread when dropped from tip of spoon or tines of silver fork. Pour syrup gradually on beaten white of egg, beating mixture constantly, and continue beating until of right consistency to spread; then add flavoring and pour over cake, spreading evenly with back of spoon. Crease as soon as firm. If not beaten long enough, frosting will run; if beaten too long, it will not be smooth. Frosting beaten too long may be improved by adding a few drops of lemon juice or boiling water. This frosting is soft inside, and has a glossy surface. If frosting is to be ornamented with nuts or candied cherries, place them on frosting as soon as spread.

This frosting, on account of the larger quantity of egg, does not stiffen so quickly as White Mountain Cream, therefore is more successfully made by the inexperienced.

SOURCE: FARMER, 1918

Devils on Horseback

Pitted prunes
Strips of bacon
Squares of bread

Roll each prune in a small strip of bacon. Place on squares of bread and bake for 20 minutes in a moderate over (180C). Serve hot.

SOURCE: ANON

Note: Dates, liver or dried apricots can be used instead of prunes. Sometimes the fruit is stuffed with mango chutney, cheese, almonds, salted almonds or smoked oysters. Devils on Horseback can be served on toast, with watercress.

About Devils on Horseback

Dating back to Victorian England, theses canapes are a combination of sweet and savoury flavours. This dish was perhaps named with reference to another finger-food - Angels on Horseback. An advertisement in Melbourne's Argus newspaper,Saturday 12 May 1956, proclaims - "Devils on horses!FRIENDS will gallop to YOUR party if you serve Devils on Horseback - the way they should be served! All you need is: Four large prunes, hot chutney, salted almonds; two rashers of bacon, and four croûtes of fried bread or toast."

The dish was popular again in the 1970s.

The etymology can't be traced, but it is widely held that the name derives from the red (bacon)and black (prune) combination reflecting the fiery black and red colours of the devil. Others claim that the bacon wrapping around the prune represents the legs of a rider wrapped around a horse.

5
FAIRIES

Chocolate Fairy Cakes

4 oz. of butter
2 oz. grated chocolate
4 oz. Flour
2 eggs
1/2 teaspoon of baking powder
4 oz. castor sugar
Vanilla essence, glace cherries and angelica

Sift the flour and baking powder, add the chocolate and mix well.
Cream butter and sugar, add one egg and half the dry ingredients.
Add the second egg, and the rest of the dry ingredients, then the
essence. Put into small patty tins or paper cases and decorate with
cherries and angelica.
Bake in a hot oven for about 15 minutes.

"CHOCOLATE fairy cakes add a touch of colour to the after-
noon tea table."

Source: The West Australian, 1937

Fairy Biscuits

4 oz. butter
4 oz sugar
1 egg
5 oz. S.R. flour
Almonds
Half a teaspoon of vanilla essence
Half a teaspoon almond essence

Put the butter in a saucepan and beat until it becomes a light brown colour.
Take off the stove. Let it cool, but do not let it set. Beat in the sugar, then the egg, and when thoroughly mixed add the flour, sifted with a pinch of salt, and the essence.
Drop half a teaspoon of the mixture on to cold greased oven trays a little distance apart, as these biscuits spread. Place half an almond on each one and bake on a moderate oven till done.

SOURCE: TOWNSVILLE DAILY BULLETIN, QLD. 1935

Fairy Cake

With cup of sugar, take half a cup of milk, two sups of flour, two tea- spoons of baking powder, a teaspoon of essence of vanilla, and the whites of three eggs.
Beat the batter and sugar together. Add the whites of the eggs well beaten. Then add the flour and baking powder, and, lastly, the vanilla and milk. For the icing, take icing sugar.
Beat well and spread on the cake, while still in the tin and hot.

SOURCE: TOWNSVILLE DAILY BULLETIN, QLD 1927

Fairy Candles

Take quantity of ingredients according the number of candles wanted. Ingredients are, pineapple rings, bananas, & few cherries, and cream.

A slice of pineapple will be required for the base of each candle. Then put half a banana in the centre for the candle, a. small piece of candied cherry for the flame, and a little cream round the bottom of the banana, for the holder.

This dainty only takes a few minutes to prepare and is a delight to children.

'Sixth prize is awarded to Mrs. Stevens, 131 Federation-street, Mt. Hawthorn, for recipe for FAIRY CANDLES.'

SOURCE: SUNDAY TIMES, PERTH, WA 1927

Fairy Delights

Two cups flour, one cup sugar, one teaspoonful baking powder, two eggs, half-cup. butter, flavouring.

Rub the butter into the flour, mix in the baking powder, beat the eggs and sugar together and mix into a dough; knead for a few minutes, roll out very thin and cut into small rounds or fancy shapes. Bake in a quick oven.

'Fifth prize is awarded to Mrs. R. Wellstead, Bremer Bay, for recipe: FAIRY DELIGHTS.'

SOURCE: SUNDAY TIMES, PERTH, WA 1915

Fairy Gingerbread

Take 1/2 teacupful of granulated sugar, 1/4 cupful melted butter, 1/2 cupful treacle, in which dissolve 1 teaspoonful of soda, 1/2 cupful sour milk, 1 teaspoonful ginger, 1/4 teaspoonful cinnamon, 1 1/2 cupfuls flour. This will not be very stiff, but do not add more flour or it will not be light and fluffy.

Third prize is awarded to Miss R Laurisson, York-road, Bellevue, for recipe for: FAIRY GINGERBREAD.

SOURCE: SUNDAY TIMES, PERTH, WA 1921

Fairy Shortbread

3 breakfast cups plain flour
1 breakfast cup cornflour,
2 level teaspoons baking powder,
A pinch of salt,
1 breakfast cup icing sugar,
1 pound butter
2 eggs, essence as liked,
Nuts or cherries to decorate

Pass all dry ingredients through sifter, mixing well. Rub in the butter next; then add the eggs, beaten slightly, and any essence preferred. Now "with the hand" clutch all into a solid mass till very smooth (the warmth of the hand works wonders with the apparently impossible). Should the mixture become at all sticky set aside in a cool place until it can be easily rolled between the hands, and will leave the mixture bowl quite clean.

Roll the mixture into small balls (about the size of a small walnut) between the hands, and set well apart on cold oven tray. Now, say you have used lemon or almond essence, in that case press half a walnut or blanched almond into the little balls be fore placing them in the oven.

With French rose or vanilla essence, press a piece of candied or cocktail cherry well into the little shortbreads, the cut or sharp edge helps it to stay in place.

Be sure you leave plenty of room between each shortbread, for they spread amazingly. Bake, till just tinted lightly, in a moderate oven about 1/4 hour. Yields about 6 1/2 dozen shortbreads, which will keep well for months in an airtight tin.

"MRS. BOYLE, of Brighton, prize winner in our cookery competition for SAVORY PIES, referred to on unusual recipe for FAIRY SHORTBREAD, which is one of her family's favourites. There have been many inquiries for this recipe, so Mrs. Boyle has very kindly passed it on to me for our readers."

SOURCE: THE ARGUS, MELBOURNE, 1950

Fairy Sponge

Four eggs,
3/4 cup sugar,
1/2 cup cornflour,
1 dessertspoon plain flour
1 teaspoon cream of tartar,
1/2 teaspoon bicarb. soda,
Pinch of salt.

Beat the whites of the eggs first, then add sugar, and beat until it melts. Add yolks of eggs. and beat for a few minutes, then lightly mix in tbs sifted dry ingredients.

Line sandwich tins with well buttered paper, putting two thicknesses in bottom of tins. Divide mixture into the tins, and bake in a moderate oven about 10 minutes. This sponge is too light to ice, but is delicious with whipped cream between.

SOURCE: CAIRNS POST, QLD, 1940

Fairy Wells

1 cup butter
1/2 cup sugar,
1 egg
1/3rd cup of milk
Essence to flavour
1 cup desiccated cocoanut (sic)
6 cups self-raising flour

Cream butter and sugar, add egg, beat well, and add essence and cocoanut ; mix well together, add flour ; turn on to floured board, knead and roll out in a thin layer.

Cut into small rounds, put half of them on a floured tin, and bake in a moderately hot oven until a nice brown colour. In the centre of each of the other discs cut a hole 1/2 in. in diameter, and bake as before.

When cold join one disc of each kind together by spreading jam between. Ice the top, sprinkle with cocoanut, and fill the hole in the centre with jam.

Any icing may be used. These biscuits keep for a long time.

SOURCE: MORNING BULLETIN, QLD.1930
'Cooks' Corner: "Jolly Madcap" Is Responsible For This Delicious Sounding Recipe.

Strawberry Fairy Pudding

Two eggs
1 dessertspoon shortening
1 tablespoon sugar
Vanilla essence
1 1/2 cups cake cake crumbs
1 pint milk
1 cup hulled strawberries
2 extra tablespoons sugar.

Separate yolks and whites of eggs. Cream the shortening and sugar, add vanilla essence and egg yolks, beating well. Soak the cake crumbs in the milk and   add to mixture. Two-thirds fill pie dish with this mixture and bake in moderate oven till custard is set. Roll the strawberries in castor sugar and place on top of custard. Beat egg whites and extra sugar till very stiff, and place on strawberries. Bake in oven till a light brown. Garnish with strawberries. When straw berries are out of season, other fruit can be used

SOURCE: WORKER, BRISBANE, QLD, 1949
'Mrs. P. Cornwell, Tiaro, N.C. Line Wins 'Best Recipe For Week Ended October 17, 1949

6

FOOD ATTACKS

In Ambush - Apricots

1 oz. gelatine
1 quart milk
3 eggs
1 cup of sugar
Apricots, cooked but not mushy.

Soak gelatine in a little of the milk. Dissolve in the rest of the milk to which sugar has been added. When nearly boiling pour over the beaten eggs.
Return to stove to thicken custard, but do not boil. Pour into a wetted mould, having first flavored to taste.
When firm, carefully scoop out the centre. Put in the apricots.
Melt the scooped-out cream and pour back over apricots.
Leave till set.
Peaches, strawberries, plums, or any other seasonable fruits may be used for this pudding.

SOURCE: BARRIER MINER, BROKEN HILL, NSW 1936

In Ambush - Cherries

1 pint milk
3 eggs
1/2 cup sugar
Juice 1 lemon
1/2 lb. preserved cherries
1 oz. sheet gelatine
Vanilla to taste

Soak gelatine in the milk 1 hour, add sugar and the yolks of eggs, well beaten.
Put in a double saucepan, put over the fire and stir all the time. Do not let it boil.
When like boiled custard, remove from the fire, and when it begins to set beat the whites of the eggs to a stiff foam.
Beat all well together and pour into a wet mould to set.
Then cut out an oblong hole in the shape, put in the cherries which have been soaked in hot water with some liquor or brandy, if liked. Return over them what you cut out and set again; see that the cherries are quite hidden.

SOURCE: BARRIER MINER, BROKEN HILL, NSW 1937

In Ambush - Orange Jelly

Cut oranges in halves lengthwise, remove pulp and juice.
With juice make Orange Jelly to fill half the pieces. Fill remaining pieces with Charlotte Russe mixture (see recipe for Icy Bomb). When both are firm, put together in pairs and tie together with narrow white ribbon.

SOURCE: FARMER, 1918

In Ambush - Pears

Take one stewed pear for each person, one pint of raspberry jelly, and one gill of cream. Stew pears gently and whole. When jelly is cool enough pour over the pears. Whip the cream, and when jelly is set, place this over the top with a few blanched almonds cut in strips or halved.

SOURCE: THE REGISTER, ADELAIDE, 1925

In Ambush - Peas

Get as many [bread] rolls as required. Cut off the tops for lids and remove the crumbs. Fill the cases with the following mixture:
Put half a pint of milk in a clean pan; add one cupful of cold cooked peas, pepper and salt to taste, and 1 oz. of butter.
When boiling remove from the fire, and stir in one well-beaten egg. Pour into cases and put on the lids and stand upright in a tin. These are delicious for picnics.

SOURCE: SUNDAY TIMES, PERTH, WA 1916

7

IS THIS THING EDIBLE?

Bee-sting Cake

Dough
1 1/2 cups plain flour
1/4 cup cornflour
1 tablespoon active dry yeast
2 tablespoons sugar
1 pinch salt
3/4 cup lukewarm milk
3 tablespoons butter

Almond Topping
3 tablespoons butter
1 1/2 tablespoons icing sugar
1 tablespoon milk
5/8 cup sliced almonds
1 tablespoon honey (optional)

Custard Filling
1 1/2 cups milk
1/3 cup cornflour
1 tablespoon sugar
1 egg, beaten
1 teaspoon almond essence
1 cup whipping cream
1/2 tablespoon cream of tartar

Combine flour, yeast, 2 tablespoons sugar, salt, 3/4 cup milk, and 3 tablespoons butter or margarine. Turn dough out onto a lightly floured surface. Knead until smooth and elastic, about 15 to 20 minutes. Place in a well greased bowl, and cover. Let rise in a warm place for 1 hour, or until doubled.

Punch down the dough. Roll out to a 5cm thickness. Spread into a greased 8 inch square baking pan. Cover, and let rise for 30 minutes.

Melt 3 tablespoons butter or margarine and icing sugar in a saucepan. Add almonds and 1 tablespoon milk. Remove from heat, and stir in honey. Spread evenly and carefully onto the dough. Allow dough to continue to rise for an additional 30 minutes.
Bake at 205 degrees C (400 degrees F) for 20 to 25 minutes, or until crust turns golden brown. Cool on a wire rack.

Dissolve cornstarch in a little milk. Combine 1 1/2 cups milk, cornflour, and 1 tablespoon sugar in the top of a double boiler. Heat while stirring until thickened, about 2 to 3 minutes. Add in beaten egg, and keep stirring for about 2 more minutes, or until thick. Remove from heat, and stir in extract. Chill, covered, in refrigerator for at least 1 hour. Beat the whipping cream with the cream of tartar until stiff. Fold into the chilled pudding.

Cut the cooled almond crust bread into 3 x 5 cm rectangles. Slice each horizontally into halves. Fill with pudding mixture. Chill, and serve cold.

SOURCE: ANON

About Bee-Sting Cake
Bienenstich or Bee sting cake is a German dessert made of a sweet yeast dough with a baked-on topping of caramelized almonds and filled with a vanilla custard, Buttercream or cream.
The cake may have earned its name from its honey topping: according to one legend, a bee was attracted to it, and the baker who invented the cake was stung.
Another source cites a legend of German bakers from the 15th century who lobbed beehives at raiders from a neighboring village, successfully repelling them, and celebrated later by baking a version of this cake named after their efforts.

SOURCE: WIKIPEDIA

Bedfordshire Clanger

450g pre-made shortcrust pastry
1 egg, beaten
2 tsp granulated sugar

For the savoury filling:
1 small onion, chopped
1 tbsp lard
225g minced pork
1 tsp dried sage
1 cooking apples
50g cooked peas
salt and fresh ground black pepper

For the sweet filling:
2 dessert apples
50g Dates, stoned and chopped
grated rind of 1 orange
55g sultanas
2 tbsp caster sugar

Preheat the oven to 220°C/gas 7.
To make the savoury filling, place the chopped onion and lard in
a frying pan over a medium heat for 2-3 minutes, until the onion
is soft and golden. Stir in the pork and sage and cook gently for 5
minutes, stirring often.
Peel, core and chop the apple and add it to the pork mixture. Cook
for a further 5 minutes, then stir in the peas, season to taste and
leave to cool.
To make the sweet filling, peel and chop the apples, then place in
a mixing bowl and stir in the chopped dates, orange rind, sultanas
and sugar. Roll out the pastry to about 5mm thick and cut out two
circles, 25cm in diameter.

Re-roll the trimmings and cut out two thick 12.5 x 1cm strips of pastry. Brush the long edges of each strip with a little beaten egg, and stand one strip, on its long side, from the edge to the centre of each circle, to form a wall. Make the strip stand up by pressing the bottom edge quite firmly onto the circle. Brush the edges of the circles all the way around with beaten egg.

On one side of each pastry wall put half of the savoury filling, and on the other side put half of the sweet filling.

Fold the other half of each pastry circle over the filling to form a pasty shape, and press the centre lightly so that the dividing strip sticks to the top.

Pinch the edges firmly together, brush each clanger with the rest of the beaten egg and sprinkle with sugar.

Bake the clangers in the preheated oven for 15 minutes, then lower the heat to 190°C/gas 5 and bake for a further 25 minutes. Serve hot.

SOURCE: BEDFORD BOROUGH COUNCIL

About Bedfordshire Clanger

The Bedfordshire Clanger is a dish from the county of Bedfordshire, in England. It is an elongated suet crust dumpling with a savoury filling at one end and a sweet filling at the other comprising a main course and dessert in one package.

The savoury end is traditionally meat with diced potatoes and vegetables (although a filling without meat is also possible), and the sweet end is usually jam, or sweetened apple or other fruit. Traditionally the top pasty is scored with a few lines to denote the sweet end.

Historically, the Bedfordshire Clanger was made by women for their husbands to take to their agricultural work as a midday meal. The dish is still available at various bakers and served at some hotels, restaurants and local places of interest.

SOURCE: WIKIPEDIA

Bomb-Shell

1 1/2 lb steak cut in small pieces and rolled in the following mixture - 1/4 teaspoon Pepper, 1 teaspoonful Salt, 2 teaspoonsful Flour. To make the Paste:- 1 lb Flour, 1 teaspoonful Carbonate of Soda, 1 teaspoonful Cream of Tartar, 2 oz Butter, a little Pepper and Salt.

Mix with a little milk into a firm paste, then cut in two pieces, 1 large and 1 small piece. Roll out large piece into a round scone. Put the steak in centre and gather up the paste. Put a little water inside; roll out the small piece and put it on top; tie in a pudding-cloth and boil for 3 hours. This is very appetising and economical.

SOURCE: ANON, 1820

Card Cakes

1/3 cup butter
Jordan almonds
1 cup powdered sugar
1 tablespoon breakfast cocoa
2 eggs
2 tablespoons sugar
1 cup flour
1/4 teaspoon powdered cinnamon
1/3 teaspoon salt
1/4 teaspoon vanilla
Shredded cocoanut

Cream the butter, add sugar, eggs well beaten, flour, and salt. Spread mixture on bottom of a buttered inverted dripping-pan, decorate with almonds blanched and cut in strips, and bake in slow oven. Cut in desired shape, using heart, spade, and diamond shaped cutters before removing from pan. To give variety, divide mixture in halves. To one-half add sugar, cocoa, cinnamon, and vanilla, then spread on pan and sprinkle with shredded cocoanut (sic).

SOURCE: FARMER, 1918

Copper Pennies

2 lbs. carrots, thinly sliced to resemble copper coins
1 green pepper, thinly sliced (half rounds)
1 cup celery, sliced
1 onion, thinly sliced (also half rounds)
2/3 cup sugar
1 tsp. Worcestershire sauce
1 can tomato soup
1/2 cup vegetable oil
2/3 cup cider vinegar
1 tsp. prepared mustard
salt and pepper to taste

Cook carrots in salted boiling water until cooked, but still crisp.
Rinse in cold water.
Arrange layers of carrots, celery, green pepper and onion in a
non-metal container.
Combine all remaining ingredients in a saucepan, bring to the boil,
stirring until thoroughly blended.
Pour marinade over carrots but do not stir.
Cover with a tightly fitting lid and refrigerate until flavor is absorbed (at least 12 hours).
Will keep for several weeks in the refrigerator.

SOURCE: ANON

Cold Cabinet Pudding

1/4 box gelatine or 1 tablespoon granulated gelatine
1/3 cup sugar
1/8 teaspoon salt
1/4 cup cold water
1 teaspoon vanilla
2 cups scalded milk
1 tablespoon brandy
Yolks 3 eggs
5 lady fingers
6 macaroons

Soak gelatine in cold water and add to custard made of milk, eggs, sugar, salt; strain, cool slightly, and flavor with vanilla and brandy. Place a mould in pan of ice-water, decorate with candied cherries and angelica, cover with mixture, added carefully by spoonfuls; when firm, add layer of lady fingers (first soaked in custard), then layer of macaroons (also soaked in custard); repeat, care being taken that each layer is firm before another is added. Garnish, and serve with Cream Sauce I and candied cherries.

Cream Sauce I
3/4 cup thick cream
1/3 cup powdered sugar
1/4 cup milk
1/2 teaspoon vanilla

Mix cream and milk, beat until stiff, using egg-beater; add sugar and vanilla.

SOURCE: FARMER, 1918

About Cold Cabinet Pudding

There are many variants of cabinet pudding, hot, cold, and even made with ice cream. The political link, though unexplained, is constant. Ude (1828) gives, as an alternative name, *poudin à la chancelière.* Another name is Diplomat pudding, which may just be a translation of the French Pouding à la diplomate. Only the names differ; the puddings are all alike.

The general method is to grease a pudding basin; stick currants or glacé fruit to the grease; line it with sponge fingers or soaked macaroons; and then fill this lining with layers of dried fruit, sponge fingers, and custard (in cold versions including gelatin). Most versions include some spirit or liqueur as a flavouring. Hot ones are boiled; cold ones are made with a custard or cream that needs no further cooking.

SOURCE: ALAN DAVIDSON IN HUFFINGTON POST FOOD ENCYCLOPEDIA

Frangipani Cake

'Fran ·gi ·pan ·i/ franj panē/ Noun: A tropical American tree or shrub (genus Plumeria) of the dogbane family, with clusters of fragrant white, pink, or yellow flowers. Perfume obtained from this plant.

'

400g almond paste cut into small pieces
1 cup sugar
1 cup butter, at room temperature
6 eggs, at room temperature
3/4 cup cake flour
1/4 cup cornflour

Preheat oven to 180°C with rack in middle. Grease and flour a small cake pan. Sift together the cornflour and plain flour
With electric mixer on low speed, blend almond paste, sugar and butter.
Continue mixing, adding eggs one at a time. Beat on high until batter is light and fluffy, about 3 minutes.
Carefully fold in the sifted flours. Gently fold into batter until just blended. Spread batter evenly into pan.
Bake 30-35 minutes or until golden and the cake's top springs back when lightly touched.

SOURCE: ANON

Frangipan Tart

Short crust
Eight eggs,
3oz butter,
3oz sugar,
1/2 oz flour,
One pint milk
Two bay leaves,
Four or six fine strips lemon rind,
Nutmeg.

Mix the flour with a little milk Simmer rest of milk with the bay leaves, lemon rind and two pinches of nutmeg for about 15 minutes, then strain it and blend with the flour and milk.

Return to saucepan, add the butter, sugar, and slightly beaten eggs and stir over a low heat until it thickens, do not let it boil.

Line a tart tin with the paste, pour in the filling when cool and bake for about 30 minutes. Serve cold decorated with whipped cream and crystallised cherries.

If bay leaves are not available, use a few drops of vanilla essence.

SOURCE: THE ARGUS, MELBOURNE, 1936

Haystack Savoury

Prepare 1 pint of cooked young green peas and 1 lb. of cooked, mashed and creamed potatoes. On a serving plate mould a potato ring of the hot mashed potatoes, fill centre with drained seasoned peas. Place in oven and keep hot. To prepare the straws, peel and thinly cut 3 medium sized potatoes into straws (like matches). Wash, drain and dry. Cook in clear, very hot fat till a pale amber color. Smooth sides of potato ring and spread the straws evenly all over the top and sides to resemble a haystack. Chop 1 table-spoon of parsley and sprinkle round foot to imitate grass. Serve with mixed grill and tomato sauce or lamb cutlets.

SOURCE: BARRIER MINER, BROKEN HILL, NSW 1939
'Ways Of Serving Potatoes - Mrs. Hocking Wins First Prize
'FIRST prize in this week's recipe contest was awarded to Mrs. M. E. Hocking, of South Road, for her "Haystack Savory" recipe.
Mrs. F. Hobb, of 239 Cummins Lane, was second, and Mrs. C. Tisher, of 234 Morgan Street, was third. The subject was "New and Novel Ways of Serving Potatoes."

Haystacks - Coconut

Six tablespoons coconut,
4 tablespoons sugar,
1 egg

Mix all ingredients together in basin. Press mixture into wetted eggcup, then turn out on to greased oven slide. Continue in this manner until all mixture is used. Bake in moderate oven 10 to 12 minutes. Loosen with spatula, let cool on tray.

SOURCE: THE AUSTRALIAN WOMEN'S WEEKLY 1933
Consolation prize of one pound to Mrs. J. Wilkinson, "Cornforth," 10 Hertford St., Berkeley, N.S.W.

Horseshoes -Almond I

1/4 lb.flour,
1/4 lb ground rice,
1/4 lb.ground almonds,
1/4 lb. butter,
1/4 lb castor sugar,
2 egg yolks,
About 2 dozen almonds.

Cream the butter and sugar,and thoroughly mix with dry ingredients. Bind together with egg yolks, then, when mixed to a stiff paste, roll this out; and cut into narrow strips about 4 in. long by 1 in. wide.
Make these into horseshoes, and stud them at intervals with chopped, blanched almonds, to serve as imitation nails, or they can be sprinkled all over with finely chopped almonds.
Place the horseshoes on rice paper- in a buttered tin, and bake for 20 minutes in a moderate oven.

SOURCE: SUNDAY TIMES, PERTH, 1927

Horseshoes - Almond II

10 oz. almond paste
White 1 egg
5 oz. confectioners' sugar   (icing sugar)
1/2 teaspoon cinnamon
Chocolate frosting
Red frosting freshly made of white of one egg and two-thirds cup confectioners' sugar and a few drops of red food colouring, beaten together until stiff enough to spread.

Work together almond paste and sugar on a smooth board or marble slab. Then add whites of eggs gradually, and work until mixture is perfectly smooth. Confectioners at first use the hand, afterwards a palette knife, which is not only of use for mixing but for keeping board clean.

Dredge a board with sugar, knead mixture slightly, and shape in a long roll. Pat, and roll one-fourth inch thick, using a rolling-pin. After rolling the piece should be four inches wide. Spread with freshly made red frosting.

Cut in strips four inches long by three-fourths inch wide. This must be quickly done, as a crust soon forms over frosting. To accomplish this, use two knives, one placed through mixture where dividing line is to be made, and the other used to make a clean sharp cut on both sides of first knife.

Knives should be kept clean by wiping on a damp cloth. Remove strips as soon as cut, to a tin sheet, greased with lard and then floured.

Cut in strips six inches long by one-half inch wide. As soon as cut, shape quickly, at the same time carefully, in form of horseshoes. Bake twenty minutes on centre grate in a slow oven.

When cool, make eight dots with chocolate frosting to represent nails.

SOURCE: FARMER 1918

Horseshoes- Plain

One pound plain flour.
6 oz. sugar,
6 oz. butter,
2 or 3 eggs,
1 teaspoon baking powder,
A little milk,
Good pinch salt.

Sift flour, baking powder, and salt, cream, butter, and sugar, and add gradually the beaten eggs, next add the flour and sufficient milk to make a firm dough.

Use as required for: -- 1. Horseshoes (for luck). -- Roll out mixture thinly and cut into strips 1/2 in. x 5 in. Shape each into a horse-shoe. Press small pieces of glace cherry or almond into form of 'nails.' Bake in a moderate oven 10 to 15 minutes.

SOURCE: THE MAIL, ADELAIDE, SA 1941

Ice-box Pie

Eight sweet biscuits,
1/4 lb. melted butter,
1 tin sweetened condensed milk,
1/2 cup lemon juice,
1 egg,
2 tablespoons sugar.

Crush biscuits and mix with melted butter to make a biscuit crust and line 8in. pie dish with it. (Use more biscuits and butter for a thicker crust.)

Blend condensed milk, yolk of egg, and lemon juice to make filling; pour over crust.

Whip white of egg and a little sugar to a meringue and place on top 1 of the lemon filling. Cook in oven until I meringue is lightly browned and then place in refrigerator until cold. This dessert improves if left overnight in refrigerator.

Serves 6 to 8.

SOURCE: THE AUSTRALIAN WOMEN'S WEEKLY 1950

About Ice-Box Pie

Ice-box Pies (also known as Refrigerator Pies) are no-bake recipes that became popular during the Great Depression. Dozens of recipe variations exist. Crusts range from a standard pastry shell to crushed cracker and cookie crumb-crusts.

Icy Bomb (also known as Bombe Glacée)

Line a mould with sherbet or water ice; fill with ice cream or thin Charlotte Russe mixture; cover, pack in salt and ice, and let stand two hours.

The mould may be lined with ice cream. Pomegranate or Raspberry Ice and Vanilla or Macaroon Ice Cream make a good combination.

Charlotte Russe Mixture
1/4 box gelatine or 1 tablespoon granulated gelatine
1/3 cup powdered sugar
3 1/2 cups thin cream, whipped
1/4 cup cold water
1 1/2 teaspoons vanilla
1/3 cup scalded cream

Soak gelatine in cold water, dissolve in scalded cream, strain into a bowl, and add sugar and vanilla. Set bowl in pan of ice-water and stir constantly until it begins to thicken, then fold in whip from cream, adding one-third at a time. Should gelatine mixture become too thick, melt over hot water, and again cool before adding whip.

SOURCE: FARMER, 1918

About Icy Bomb

A bombe glacée or simply a bombe in English, is an ice cream dessert frozen in a spherical mould so as to resemble a cannonball, hence the name. Escoffier gives over sixty recipes for bombes in 'Le Guide Culinaire'. The dessert appeared on restaurant menus as early as 1882.

SOURCE: WIKIPEDIA

Imperial Sticks in Rings (Soup Garnish)

Cut stale bread in one-third inch slices, remove crusts, spread thinly with butter, and cut slices in one-third inch strips and rings; put in pan and bake until delicately browned. Arrange three sticks in each ring.

SOURCE: FARMER 1918

Impossible Pie

1/2 cup self-raising flour
1 3/4 cups sugar
4 eggs
2 cups milk
1 3/4 cups sugar
1/2 cup melted butter
1 tablespoon vanilla
200g desiccated coconut

Mix sugar with flour and set aside. Beat the eggs well. Add milk to beaten eggs, then stir in melted butter, vanilla and coconut. Pour mixture into two greased pie dishes 23 cm in diameter. Bake at 180 C for 30 to 40 minutes.

Source: Anon

About Impossible Pie
Also known as Mystery Pie and Amazing Pie, this 20th century dish gets its name from the fact that the pie crust forms by itself, and does not have to be made separately. After you pour the mixture into the baking dish, the layers naturally settle into a pie configuration, with the crust on the bottom and the filling on the top. This simple basic recipe can be used for making sweet dessert pies or savoury meat, vegetable and cheese pies.

Malaga Boats

Roll puff or plain paste one-eighth inch thick, line individual boat-shaped tins, prick, and half fill with rice or barley to keep pastry in desired shape. Bake in a hot oven. Remove from tins and cover bottom of boats with marmalade, and on marmalade arrange three or four malaga grapes cooked in syrup five minutes. For the syrup boil one-half cup, each, sugar and water five minutes.

Source: Farmer, 1918

Marble Cake

Black Cake: One cupful of brown sugar, half-cupful of molasses, half-cupful of butter, half-cupful of buttermilk, two cupfuls of flour, yolks of four eggs, one teaspoonful of Baking Powder, one teaspoonful of cinnamon, cloves, allspice and nutmeg mixed.

White Cake: The whites of four eggs, half-cupful of butter, half-cupful of buttermilk, two cupfuls of flour, two of sugar, one teaspoonful of baking powder.

Pour a layer of white mixture into the cake tin, then a layer of black mixture, and so on alternately, and bake in a moderate oven until the top of the cake bounces back when lightly touched in the middle.

Source: Howson, 1881

Mud Pie I

Measure into saucepan 1/4 cup ground chocolate, and stir in 3 cups milk. Heat until chocolate melts.

Break into mixing bowl 3 eggs, beat slightly, and beat in 1-3rd cup plus one tablespoon sugar, 1/4 teaspoon salt, 1 teaspoon vanilla (or 1/2 teaspoon nutmeg).

Add milk mixture to egg mixture and pour immediately into pan lined with raw pastry which has been chilled in refrigerator for 1 hour. Bake in hot oven 10 to 15 minutes at first to brown crust, then reduce to moderate oven 30 to 35 minutes to finish baking custard.

Source: Northern Times, Carnarvon, WA 1939

Mud Pie II

Line a plate with good pastry. Take 1/2 pint of milk or 1 cup, 2 tablespoons sugar, 1 tablespoon cornflour, 1 table spoon butter, 1 tablespoon cocoa, 2 eggs.

Dissolve cocoa in milk and bring to a boil, mix cornflour to a smooth paste with a little cold milk and stir into boiling mixture.

Take off stove, add butter and beaten egg yolk and sugar. Pour into pastry and bake in fairly hot oven until pastry is cooked.

Beat whites of eggs stiff, then fold in 3 tablespoons sugar, spread on top and bake till golden brown.

Source: Worker, Brisbane, Qld. 1939

Neapolitan Baskets

Bake sponge cake in gem pans, cool, and remove centres to create 'baskets'. Fill with Cream Sauce I, flavouring half the sauce with chocolate.

Cream Sauce I
3/4 cup thick cream
1/3 cup powdered sugar
1/4 cup milk
1/2 teaspoon vanilla

Mix cream and milk, beat until stiff, using egg-beater; add sugar and vanilla. Melt chocolate, dilute with hot water, cool, and add half of Cream Sauce slowly to chocolate.
After filling, garnish with candied cherries and angelica and insert strips of angelica to represent handles.

SOURCE: FARMER, 1918

Omnibus Pudding
Ingredients. 3 ozs. of flour, 3 ozs. of finely-chopped suet, 3 ozs. of stoned raisins, 2 ozs. of golden syrup warmed, of a pint of milk.
Method. Mix all the ingredients thoroughly together, pour into a well-buttered basin, and steam for 2 hours. Serve with a suitable sauce.
Time. 2\ hours. Average Cost, 4|d. Sufficient for 3 or 4 persons.

SOURCE: MRS BEETON

Seafoam Candy

450g white sugar
240ml water
4 tablespoons distilled white vinegar
3 tablespoons light corn syrup
1/2 teaspoon baking soda
340g semi-sweet chocolate chips
2 tablespoons shortening
30g square unsweetened chocolate

Grease a 20cm square baking pan; set aside.

Put sugar, vinegar, syrup, and water in a heavy 4 litre saucepan (cast iron if you have it).

Gently heat the mixture, stirring with a wooden spoon, until sugar has dissolved and syrup has melted. Bring to a boil, cover and boil for 3 minutes, then remove lid and boil until temperature reaches 140 degrees C (285 degrees F) on a candy thermometer.

Remove from heat and stir in the baking soda, mixing well to allow bubbles to subside a little.

Pour hot mixture into prepared pan and leave until just beginning to set. Mark into squares with a lightly oiled knife. Leave to set completely.

Cut or break into pieces.

Combine chocolate chips, shortening, and baking chocolate in a 2-quart glass bowl. Melt in a double saucepan over simmering water. Stir with a wooden spoon. Dip candy pieces into chocolate, covering completely. Allow to cool on waxed paper.

Wrap pieces individually in waxed paper, twisting the ends together, and store in an airtight container.

SOURCE: ANON

Seafoam in a Honey Roll

Honey Roll

Beat 3 eggs till very light and frothy. Then add à cup of sugar and beat 15 minutes. Stir in 1 tablespoon of melted, but not heated, honey. Sift 1 cup of arrowroot with 1 level tablespoon of flour, a pinch of salt, and a teaspoon of ground cinnamon. Add a pinch of grated nutmeg. Mix all well together, pour into shallow swiss roll tins and bake for 20 minutes.

Seafoam Filling

Dissolve 1 level teaspoon of granulated gelatine in the juice of i orange and 1 dessert- spoon of cold water. Whip till frothy, and add 1/4 lb. icing sugar, a pinch of citric acid, or a few drops of vanilla essence. Spread on warm sponge. Roll up quickly and sift over castor or icing sugar.

SOURCE: BARRIER MINER, BROKEN HILL, NSW 1939

Sussex Blanket Pudding

3 cups flour
Seasoning
2 eggs, beaten
1 1/2 cups suet
8 tablespoons breadcrumbs
A little milk
(See measure conversions for more information)

Savory fillings
Liver and bacon, minced, with parsley and onion; or sausage meat; or any scraps of minced meat.

Sweet fillings
Jam or golden syrup; or mincemeat; or chopped apples, a little butter, and orange marmalade or quince jam; or finely chopped peel, currants, raisins and sugar.

Combine the dry ingredients in a large bowl. Fold in the eggs, then mix with milk to form a dough.
Roll out the dough to a medium thickness in an oblong shape. Spread it with the chosen filling, leaving a border of pastry around the edges.
Dampen and flour a large enough cotton cloth.
Gently roll up the pastry and tie it up in the floured cloth. Boil for 2 to 3 hours

SOURCE: ANON

About Sussex Blanket Pudding
This is a very traditional, economical country dish that can be used as a sweet or savoury dish. In some areas the pudding was actually made sweet at one end and savoury at the other with a pastry divider in the middle.

War Cake

2 eggs
3/4 cup sugar
4 oz. nutro oil
1/2 lb. self-raising flour
3/4 cup boiling water.
1/4 lb. dates (chopped)
Walnuts

1/2 teaspoon carbonate of soda. Beat eggs and sugar well, then beat in the oil; add dates and lastly flour. Pour the water over dates and allow to stand until cold. Add carbonate of soda when cold. Bake for three quarters of an hour in a moderate oven in an orange cake tin. Oven at 450 degrees and turn on low at bottom.

SOURCE: THE MERCURY HOBART, TASMANIA 1945

Zeppelins in a Cloud (See also 'Bangers and Mash')

'Zeppelins in a Cloud' and 'Bangers and Mash' are both nicknames for sausages and mashed potatoes. Cook the sausages and mashed potatoes. Mound the potatoes like fluffy clouds on serving plates and place a couple of sausages on each cloud.

Mashed Potatoes.

Have them nicely boiled and steamed, and squeeze through a masher or sieve; melt 1 teaspoonful of butter in 2 tablespoonsful of milk for each pound of potatoes; add to them, and beat till smooth and white. Serve hot.

SOURCE: THE WESTERN CHAMPION AND GENERAL ADVERTISER FOR THE CENTRAL-WESTERN DISTRICTS, BARCALDINE, QLD.1905

A Nice Way to Cook Cambridge Sausages.

When you take them from the bundle, press them all to the same shape and size, prick them with a large darning needle, and bake them in a quick oven until cooked, but not overdone. Let them get cool on a cloth which will absorb the fat: roll each sausage first in beaten egg, and then in bread crumbs, and fry in enough boiling fat to cover. Serve on a very hot dish at once, garnished with small heaps of mashed potato.

SOURCE: THE QUEENSLANDER, 1905

8
MANY MOONS AGO

Half Moon Cookies

1/2 cup butter at room temperature
1 cup sugar
1 egg
1 tsp. Vanilla essence
1 cup milk
2 cup flour
1/2 tsp baking powder
1 1/2 tsp baking soda
1/2 tsp salt
1/2 cup cocoa

Mix ingredients together in the order they appear above. Beat until smooth. Drop by rounded tablespoonfuls onto greased biscuit tray, allowing 5 cm between cookies to allow for spreading.
Bake in a preheated 200° C (400°F) oven for around 7 minutes.
Allow to cool on the tray, then transfer to a wire rack to cool completely. Spread half of the flat side of each cookie with vanilla icing and half with chocolate icing. Makes about 24 cookies.

White Icing:
Combine 2 tablespoons butter, 1/2 teaspoon vanilla and 2 cups powdered sugar. Add milk and moisten.

Chocolate Icing:
Combine 2 tablespoons butter, 1/2 teaspoon vanilla and 2 cups powdered sugar, 2 tablespoons cocoa. Add milk and moisten.
Or, dip chocolate half in melted cooking chocolate.

SOURCE: ANON

About Half Moon Cookies

"A Black and White Cookie, also known as a Half and Half Cook-ie, a Drop Cake or a Half Moon, is a soft, sponge cake-like short-bread which is iced on one half with vanilla fondant, and on the other half by dark chocolate fondant. It is similar to a neenish tart, although neenish tarts contain a creamy filling, whereas a black and white cookie does not."

SOURCE: WIKIPEDIA

Moon - Apple

One pound apples
1 dessert spoon shortening
1 tablespoon breadcrumbs
4 tablespoons currants
1 tablespoon lemon Juice
2 tablespoons sugar
short pastry

Slice the apples thinly, and melt the shortening in a saucepan. Add the breadcrumbs. Fry till golden, then mix with apples. Mix in the currants, lemon juice and' sugar. Roll out 1/2 lb. short pastry thinly to oblong shape, and spread the mixture over. Place a cloth under one end and use it to help to roll the pastry like a Jam roll. Shape like a half-moon, place on a baking-dish, and glaze with milk. Bake 40 minutes in a hot oven.

SOURCE: WORKER , BRISBANE, QLD. 1947

Moons - Lemon

Take 4 oz. each of flour, butter, sugar and ground rice, one egg and the grated rind of a lemon. Mix the flour, butter, ground rice and sugar until it is a fine crumbly mixture. Then put in the lemon rind and mix with the egg. Roll thinly out and cut into half -moon shapes. Bake in a cool oven for about 15 minutes.

SOURCE: THE WEST AUSTRALIAN, 1935

Moonshine 1

This dessert combines a pretty appearance with palatable flavor, and is a convenient substitute for ice cream.

Beat the whites of six eggs in a broad plate to a very stiff froth; then add, gradually, six tablespoons of powdered sugar, beaten for not less than thirty minutes, and then beat in, after being cut into tiny pieces; one-half cup of preserved peaches; or fresh mashed peaches, or you can use one cup of jelly.

In serving, pour into each saucer some rich cream, sweetened and flavoured with vanilla, and on the cream, place a liberal portion of moonshine. This quantity is sufficient amount for eight or ten persons.

SOURCE: WILLEY, 1884

Note: For health safety reasons it would be best to make a cooked meringue rather than use whipped raw egg whites.

For variation, drizzle the dessert with a liqueur such as ratafia.

Moonshine II

Beat the whites of 6 eggs until they are stiff, then slowly add 6 tablespoons castor sugar, beating for 15 minutes.
Fold in 1 heaped tablespoon of peaches finely chopped
To serve, pour in each dish some sweetened cream flavored with vanilla and place the moonshine on the cream.
Serves 6 people.

SOURCE: BERLIN 1906

Note: You may wish to substitute cooked meringue for raw eggs, for health reasons.

Moonshine Cake

Whites 10 eggs
Yolks 7 eggs
1/4 teaspoon salt
1 1/2 cups sugar
7/8 teaspoon cream of tartar
1 teaspoon almond extract
1 cup pastry flour

Add salt to whites of eggs and beat until light. Sift in cream of tartar and beat until stiff. Beat yolks of eggs until thick and lemon colored and add two heaping tablespoons beaten whites. To remaining whites add gradually sugar measured after five siftings. Add almond extract and combine mixtures. Cut and fold in flour, measured after five siftings.
Bake in angel-cake pan, first dipped in cold water, in a slow oven one hour. Have a pan of hot water in oven during the baking. Cover with Maraschino Frosting.

Maraschino Frosting
1 1/2 cups sugar
one-half teaspoon cream of tartar
Whites 2 eggs
1/2 cup water
1/2 teaspoon vanilla
Maraschino to taste

Put sugar, cream of tartar and water in saucepan, and stir to prevent sugar from adhering to saucepan; heat gradually to boiling-point, and boil without stirring until syrup will thread when dropped from tip of spoon or tines of silver fork.

Pour syrup gradually on beaten white of egg, beating mixture constantly, and continue beating until of right consistency to spread; then add Maraschino flavoring and pour over cake, spreading evenly with back of spoon.

Crease as soon as firm. If not beaten long enough, frosting will run; if beaten too long, it will not be smooth.

Frosting beaten too long may be improved by adding a few drops of lemon juice or boiling water.

This frosting is soft inside, and has a glossy surface. If frosting is to be ornamented with nuts or candied cherries, place them on frosting as soon as spread.

After frosting, sprinkle with almonds blanched, shredded, and baked until delicately browned.

SOURCE: FARMER, 1918

Moonshine Pudding I

Put into a baking dish a layer of very thin bread and butter, strewed over with currants and sweetmeats, and so on till the dish is full. Mix together a pint and a half of cream, the yolks of six eggs, half a grated nutmeg, and some sugar. Pour the mixture on the top of the pudding, and bake it three quarters of an hour.

SOURCE: EATON, 1823.

Moonshine Pudding II

24 passionfruits
½ pound sugar
¾ oz gelatin
1 egg white

Scoop out the passionfruits and boil with enough water to make a pint when strained. Add the sugar and gelatin and bring to the boil. Strain into a basin and when beginning to set beat it for 20 minutes until light and frothy.
Add the well-beaten egg white to the mixture and put into a mould to set. Serve with cream.

SOURCE: ANON

Note: For health safety reasons it would be best to make a cooked meringue rather than use whipped raw egg whites

9

SIMPLY STRANGE

Bubble and Squeak I

Take the remains of cold corned beef, cold potatoes, cabbage, salt and pepper. Cut the corned beef into very small pieces and fry; put on a dish and fry the cabbage and potatoes In a little butter and season to taste; place the vegetables over the meat and serve very hot.

SOURCE: MIRROR, PERTH, WA 1934

Bubble and Squeak II

Take one pound of sliced beef (cold) about one and a half pound chopped potatoes, the same of cabbage, a little butter, pepper and salt. The vegetables must be boiled previously and cold. Fry same and keep aside hot.
Fry the beef, then add the vegetables in layers, or serve separate with the beef. Country people especially like this dish because it is easily and quickly cooked.

SOURCE: EVELYN OBSERVER AND BOURKE EAST RE-CORD , VIC 1915

About Bubble and Squeak
The term 'Bubble and Squeak' was originally coined to indicate a dish of assorted leftovers, fried together in the same pan. The term derives from the bubbling sound of the dish while cooking.

Depression Cake

Take 1 cup of dripping, sugar, currants, sultanas, and hot water. To these add 1/2 packet mixed spice, 1/2 teaspoon ground ginger, and [candied citrus] peel to taste, boil all together for 5 minutes. When mixture has cooled add 2 1/2 cups flour, 1 teaspoon carbonate of soda dissolved in hot water, mix well, and put in a tin with three layers of greased paper. Bake in moderate oven for 1 1/2 to 2 hours. Makes a rich, dark cake; will keep for weeks in air tight tin.

SOURCE: CAIRNS POST 1933

About Depression Cake

Depression cake is a type of cake that was commonly made during the Great Depression. The ingredients include little or no milk, sugar, butter or eggs, because they were then either expensive or hard to get. Similar cakes are known as "War Cake," as they avoided ingredients that were scarce or were being conserved for the use of soldiers. A common Depression Cake is also known as "Boiled Raisin Cake," or "Milkless, Eggless, Butterless Cake."

Fidget Pie

One lb. cooking apples
3/4 lb streaky bacon
1/2 lb onions
Pastry crust.

Place a layer of sliced apples at the bottom of a pie-dish. On to this place a layer of sliced onions, followed by layer of well-seasoned bacon cut into dice.

Repeat until dish is full, adding to each layer a sprinkling of pepper and salt. A small quantity of water should be .added. Cover with good, pastry crust and bake in moderate oven for two hours.

SOURCE: CAIRNS POST, 1938

Figgie Hobbin

2 oz. suet
2 oz. lard
A little milk
8 oz. flour
8 oz. dried figs
Teaspoon baking powder

Rub suet, lard. and baking powder into flour; add figs cut up finely. Mix to a stiff paste with milk.

Roll into 4 3/4 in. squares, 1/2 in. thick. Cut across the top and bake for 30 min- utes on a greased tin in a fairly hot oven.

SOURCE: WESTERN MAIL, PERTH, WA 1931

Floating Island

Separate the whites of six eggs very carefully from the yolks, and put the yolks on one side ; whisk the whites to a stiff froth. Take six tablespoonfuls of jelly and eight tablespoonfuls of powdered sugar, and beat them in the eggs gradually ; when it is stiff, pile it up in a china or glass bowl, on some cream, or on a custard made of the yolks of the eggs.

SOURCE HOWSON, 1881

Gooseberry Fool I

Poach one pound of green goose berries in some thin syrup. When they are cooked thoroughly drain them; rub them through a sieve, and collect the puree in a flat Saucepan.

Work this puree on ice and add the necessary amount of icing sugar to it. The amount of the icing sugar varies according to the acidity of the fruit and the1 sweetness of the poaching syrup.

Combine with the puree an equal quantity of very stiffly-whipped cream; set the preparation in the shape of a dome in a timbale [a baking pan]; decorate its surface by means of a piping-bag, with Chantilly cream and serve very cold. The term 'to poach' signi-fies a boiling that does not boil. The term poach is extended to all slow processes of cooking which involve the use of a liquor, however small.

Chantilly Cream
To serve 4 people use 1/2 pint cream, 1 teaspoon vanilla, 1/2 cup icing sugar. Whip the cream until it is almost stiff. Add the sugar and the vanilla when well mixed. Chill until required.

SOURCE: THE DAILY NEWS, PERTH, WA 1910

Gooseberry Fool II

Gooseberry fool is a wholesome and delicious sweet. Put a quart of gooseberries into a stewpan with a pint of water, and when they begin to turn yellow and swell, drain tho water from them and press them with the back of a spoon through a colander, sweeten them to your taste, and set them to cool. Put a quart of milk over the fire beaten up with the yolks of two eggs and a little grated nutmeg ; stir until it begins to simmer, then remove from the fire, and stir it very gradually into the cold gooseberries, let it stand until cold, and serve it. The eggs may be left out and milk only may be used if preferred.

SOURCE: LIVERPOOL HERALD, NSW 1898

Gooseberry Fool III

1 1/2 pints gooseberries
6 oz. sugar
2 table-spoonfuls water
1/4 pint cream

Top and tail the gooseberries, put the fruit, sugar, and water into a saucepan, and cook them together until quite soft. Then rub them through a fine sieve to remove pips and skins, and set them aside to cool. Beat the cream to a stiff froth, and, when the gooseberry pulp is quite cold, add it, a table-spoonful at a time, to the cream, mixing them well together. When all is added, heap the fool neatly in a silver or glass dish, and serve very cold.
Time to cook gooseberries, 15 to 20 minutes. Sufficient for 5 or 6 persons.

SOURCE: MEYER, 1898

Half-Pay Pudding I

To make the puddings, take

2 cups of self raising flour
1 pinch of salt
1 desertspoon of butter
1 cup of milk

Rub butter into flour, mix to scone dough with milk.

Make the syrup by combining in a saucepan and stirring while heating -
1 cup of hot water
1 dessertspoon of butter
1 tablespoon golden syrup
A squeeze of lemon juice

Drop the puddings into a saucepan of hot syrup and allow them to steam.
Alternatively, pour batter into a steamed-pudding basin, cover with baking paper and boil as if it was a steamed pudding.
Cook for approximately 35 minutes until firm.

Serve with vanilla custard, ice cream or cream.

SOURCE: ANON

Half-Pay Pudding II

It requires four ounces of each of the following ingredients:
Finely chopped suet flour, currants, stoned raisins, and bread-crumbs, and two ounces of sugar. Mix thoroughly with two table-spoonsful of treacle, one egg, and half-a-pint of milk.
A little salt should, of course, be added, and either mixed spice or nutmeg, according to taste.
Boil in a buttered mould for four hours, and serve with any pudding sauce.

SOURCE: THE NORTH QUEENSLAND REGISTER, 1897

Herefordshire Love in Disguise

A calf's heart
2 tablespoons shredded suet
a little mustard
2 teaspoons chopped parsley
a little lemon rind
1 tablespoon broken noodles
4 tablespoons breadcrumbs
2 tablespoons minced ham
4 or 5 slices of bacon
1 teaspoon marjoram
Seasoning
Tomato sauce
1 egg

Cook the noodles, drain and leave to get cold. Clean the calf's heart thoroughly, removing all gristle etc., wash and put in cold water for one hour.

Make a stuffing from breadcrumbs, suet, a little of the egg, herbs, mustard, seasoning, ham and lemon rind.

Dry the calf's heart, fill it with the stuffing, wrap the bacon round it and fasten with small skewers.

Wrap up loosely in foil. Place in a baking tin for 1 1/2 hours in very moderate oven or until cooked and tender. Remove the foil and brush over with egg yolk.

Then roll in breadcrumbs mixed with vermicelli. Put back in the tin and bake in the oven till nicely browned. Serve with tomato sauce

Horehound Candy

3/4 square inch pressed horehound (Marrubium vulgare)
2 cups boiling water
3 cups sugar
1/2 teaspoon cream of tartar

Pour boiling water over horehound which has been separated in pieces; let stand one minute, then strain through double cheese-cloth. Put into a granite kettle with remaining ingredients, and boil until, when tried in cold water, mixture will become brittle. Turn into a buttered pan, cool slightly, then mark in small squares. Small square packages of horehound may be bought for five cents.

Source: Farmer, 1918

Note: The herb Marrubium vulgare is considered a weed in Australia

Hygienic Soup

6 cups chicken stock
2 tablespoons butter
1/4 cup oatmeal
2 tablespoons flour
2 cups scalded milk
Salt and pepper

Heat stock to boiling-point, add oatmeal, and boil one hour; rub through sieve, add milk, and thicken with butter and flour cooked together. Season with salt and pepper.

SOURCE: FARMER 1918

Note: This soup probably received its name because the boiling sterilises the liquid.

Joe Froggers

1 cup butter
2 cups light brown sugar
1 tablespoon salt
3/4 cups water
1/4 cup dark rum
2 teaspoons baking soda
2 cups dark molasses
7 cups flour
1/2 teaspoon allspice
1 teaspoon cloves
1/2 teaspoon ginger
1/2 teaspoon ground nutmeg

Beat butter and sugar together until creamy and fluffy. Dissolve salt in water and combine with rum.

Add baking soda to molasses. Sift flour with spices. Add liquid ingredients alternately with flour mixture to butter and sugar mixture.

Stir well between additions. Dough should be sticky. Chill overnight.

In the morning, sprinkle flour on a clean pastry board, and a rolling pin. Roll dough about 1 cm thickness.

Stamp out circles with cutter. Each cookie should be the size of the inside of a coffee cup.

Bake in 190 C (375 F) degree oven between 10 and 12 minutes.

SOURCE: ANON

(See next page for more about Joe Froggers!)

About Joe Froggers

Joe Froggers are a spicy cookies that originated in Massachusetts, USA, during the colonial era. They were first made by a man known as Old Black Joe Brown and a woman called Aunt Crese, who kept a tavern on Gingerbread Hill. The cookies had a long shelf-life which made them ideal for local fishermen to take with them as provisions for long journeys at sea.

When fishermen's wives baked the cookies they would often cut their initials into each one, so that their husbands would think of them despite the miles of ocean that lay between them. The "Joe Froggers" were stored in barrels on board, often for several months, without spoiling. The high sugar content, combined with the rum acted as a preservative.

Lardy Johns

These teacakes are easy to make and are a change from tile usual tea cake. A quarter of a pound of self-raising flour, 2oz. of lard or butter, 1 dessertspoonful .sugar, 1   dessertspoonful sultanas. Rub the ingredients together and moisten with enough water to make a stiff paste.

Cut the paste cornerwise and across and bake on a floured tin for about 10 minutes. The lardy johns should be cut open and buttered, and sent to table as hot as possible.

SOURCE: SUNDAY TIMES, PERTH, WA 1925

Shoofly Pie - Dry-Bottomed
(Crumb topping is mixed into the filling)

Pie Crust:
One cup of lard
3 cups of flour
A little salt
Mix with ice-cold water into a soft dough; handle as little as possible. Roll out dough and line pie-dish with it.

Syrup for Filling
2 cups boiling water
1 cup syrup
2 teaspoonsful baking soda
Pour the boiling water over the syrup and add the soda.

Crumbs for Filling
One cup of lard
8 cups of flour
1 1/2 cups of sugar
Combine ingredients and rub together until the mixture resembles crumbs. Add the syrup and mix well.

Pour filling into pie crust and bake in a moderate oven until cooked through.

SOURCE: WORKER, BRISBANE, QLD. 1935

Shoofly Pie - Wet-Bottomed
(Soft filling and crumb topping)

3/4 cup Flour
1/2 cup brown sugar
1/2 tsp cinnamon
1/8 tsp each nutmeg, ginger, and ground cloves
1/2 tsp salt
2 tablespoons shortening
1 egg yolk, beaten well
1/2 cup barrel molasses
3/4 cup boiling water
1/2 tsp baking soda
Piecrust dough for 9-inch pie

Combine flour, sugar, spices, and salt with the shortening. Work into crumbs with your hands. Add beaten egg yolk to molasses. Pour boiling water over soda until dissolved; then add to molasses mixture. Line a 9-inch pie plate with pastry and fill it with the molasses mixture. Top with the crumb mixture. Bake at 400 degrees until the crust browns, about 10 minutes. Reduce to 325 degrees and bake firm.

SOURCE: ATTRIBUTED TO MAGDELENA HOCH KEIM OF LOBACHSVILLE, PENNSYLVANIA. (1730--?)

About Shoo-Fly Pie

According to the book 'Rare Bits: Unusual Origins of Popular Recipes', by Patricia Bunning Stevens (p. 262) shoofly pie originated when "the pie-loving Pennsylvania Dutch ...found themselves short of baking supplies in the late winter and early spring...all that was left in the pantry were flour, lard, and molasses.

From these sparse ingredients they fashioned Shoo-Fly Pie and found that their families liked it so well that they soon made it all year round.

The unusual name is presumed to come from the fact that pools of sweet, sticky molasses sometimes formed on the surface of the pie while it was cooling, inevitably attracting flies."

The term "Shoo Fly Pie", however, was not recorded in print until 1926.

SOURCE: THE ENCYCLOPEDIA OF AMERICAN FOOD & DRINK, BY JOHN MARIANI, P. 293

Star-gazy Pie

6 herrings, mackerel or pilchards
3 or 4 eggs
Tarragon vinegar
A little pepper and salt
Parsley
Breadcrumbs
Pastry

Clean and bone the fish well and season with salt, pepper and chopped parsley. Do not cut off heads. Place in a pie-dish lined with fat and breadcrumbs with heads facing inwards.
Pour 3 or 4 eggs beaten in tarragon vinegar over them.
Put a pastry over the dish (with potatoes as for pasties), leaving a hole in the middle for the heads to stick out.
Bake for about one hour in a mode- rate oven.
Place parsley into the mouths of the fish before serving.

SOURCE: WESTERN MAIL, PERTH, 1951

About Star-gazy Pie
'Stargazy Pie is a fish pie of Cornish origin. It is made with the fishes' heads sticking out of the crust all round the rim, and presumably takes its name from their appearance of gazing skywards.

In her Observer Guide to British Cookery (1984) Jane Grigson notes that 'it is a specialty of Mousehole where they make it on 23 December every year, Tom Bawcock's Eve, in memory of the fisherman who saved the town from a hungry Christmas one stormy winter'."

SOURCE: AN A-Z OF FOOD & DRINK, JOHN AYTO [OXFORD UNIVERSITY PRESS: OXFORD] 2002 (P. 323)

Tini Carlow

1 cup (180g) boiled rice
1 small onion, diced
1 cup (250g) minced meat
1 tablespoons (40ml) milk
1 tablespoon grated cheese
2 eggs, beaten
Pinch of thyme
Salt and cayenne pepper
1/2 tablespoon chopped parsley
1/2 cup (50g) dried breadcrumbs

Grease a pie dish and sprinkle with a third of the breadcrumbs, setting aside the rest of the crumbs. Mix the remaining ingredients together and f=ill the pie dish, then sprinkle the top with the reserved breadcrumbs. Bake for 30 minutes in a preheated moderate over (180C). Turn out on to a hot dish and serve with Demi-Glace brown gravy. If preferred, the mixture may be baked in ramekins for 15 to 20 minutes.

Demi Glace Brown Gravy
1 tablespoon dripping
2 cups (500 ml) beef stock
2 tablespoons flour
Salt and pepper

Melt the dripping, then remove from heat. Add flour, stir it in and brown over heat, stirring constantly. Add stock and stir until boiling and thickened. Season and serve with Tini Carlow.

SOURCE: P.W.M.U.COOKBOOK (1904)

'Tini Carlow has also been described as "Minced meat and rice with seasoning and onions baked in the oven and served with either tomato sauce or brown sauce.'
SOURCE: I-DO.COM.AU

Tipsy Pudding

Flavour Boiled Custard with Sherry wine, and pour over slices of stale sponge cake; cover with Cream Sauce I or II.

Cream Sauce I
3/4 cup thick cream
1/3 cup powdered sugar
1/4 cup milk
1/2 teaspoon vanilla

Mix cream and milk, beat until stiff, using egg-beater; add sugar and vanilla.

Cream Sauce II
1 egg
1/2 cup thick cream
1 cup powdered sugar
1/4 cup milk
1/2 teaspoon vanilla

Beat white of egg until stiff; add yolk of egg well beaten, and sugar gradually; dilute cream with milk, beat until stiff, combine mixtures, and flavour.

SOURCE: FARMER, 1918

Truffles - Chocolate

Mix well together a quarter of a cupful of sugar and 2 tablespoonfuls of self-raising: Sour; add 1 cupful of milk gradually, and cook
over a slow fire until thickened, stirring constantly; then very carefully mix in a well beaten egg yolk.
Cook a few minutes longer, then allow to cool.
Melt 1 3/4 lb. of chocolate (milk chocolate is best); beat into this
the cool custard mixture; allow to stand, overnight in a covered
container to mellow.
The next day make into small balls and roll in colored cocoanut.
This can be bought ready to use at any confectioners.

SOURCE: SUNDAY TIMES, PERTH, WA 1927
'Fourth prize is awarded to Mrs. Webb, Victoria-street Cottes-
loe Beach, for recipe for Chocolate Truffles.'

Note: The word truffle originates from the Latin for tuber, or lump

Upside-down cake - Pineapple

'Stony Creek' sends the following recipe for Pineapple Upside down Cake, which differs somewhat from recipes previously printed. '
Put table spoon and a half of butter in iron baking dish and melt.
Add half cup treacle and heat to boiling point, then remove from fire.
Strain the juice from one can of sliced pineapple and fit slices into bottom of dish.
Fill spaces between with chopped nuts and raisins.
Sift together 1 3/4 cups of flour half teaspoon bicarbonate of soda, 1 teaspoon baking powder, 1 teaspoon each of ginger and cinnamon, 1/3 teaspoon each of powdered cloves and nutmeg, and half teaspoon salt.
Cream together 3 tablespoons of butter and half cup sugar.
Stir in 1 beaten egg, and half cup treacle.
Add the dry ingredients, and mix well then add half cup boiling water and beat again.
Pour over the slices of fruit and bake for 30 - 35 minutes.
Baking tin should be well greased so that cake can be turned out easily fruit side up. This makes a delicious dessert.

SOURCE: THE ARGUS, MELBOURNE, 1936

Note: Usually, chopped fruits such as apples, pineapples and cherries are placed at the bottom of the Upside-Down Cake's pan before the batter is poured in. The cake is then baked and cooled. The fruits form a decorative topping after the cake is inverted on a serving plate and the pan is removed. The cake remains 'upside down' when served for eating.
To allow for an easier detachment, the bottom of the pan is usually covered with butter or sugar.
Traditional upside-down desserts include the American Pineapple Upside-down Cake, French Tarte Tatin, and Brazilian Bolo de Banana.

SOURCE: WIKIPEDIA

10

'RUDE' FOOD

Bangers and Mash (See also 'Zeppelins in a Cloud')

Onion Gravy
1 large onion.
1 tblspn flour.
Pepper and salt.
1 cup stock.
A little butter.

Peel, thinly slice, and fry onion in a little heated butter until golden brown. Add flour, pepper and salt. Brown the mixture then add stock and heat, stirring, until thickened. Set aside and keep warm.

Mashed Potatoes
100g butter
Salt and white pepper to season.
6 medium potatoes
100ml cream

Peel slice and cook the potatoes until soft. Place them in a bowl. Melt butter into cream and stir into potatoes. Mash with a potato masher. Season to taste and keep warm.

Sausages
8 lean sausages
2 tbsp chopped parsley for garnish

Grill sausages, spoon mash onto four plates, place two sausages on top of each mound and pour over onion gravy.
Sprinkle with chopped parsley before serving.

Black Bottom Pie I

Mix three-quarters of a cupful of sugar with two tablespoonfuls of sifted flour, and two squares of grated unsweetened chocolate, add slowly to the mixture, stirring constantly, one and a third cupfuls of scalded milk, and when it is well mixed, add the beaten yolks of two eggs, and one whole egg.
Add to the mixture, one teaspoonful of vanilla, place in a double-boiler and stir over a slow fire, until the mixture is thick and smooth, pour into a baked pie shell, cover with whipped cream, cover all over with a thick meringue, run into the oven and brown quickly.

SOURCE: LOS ANGELES TIMES, 1929

Black Bottom Pie II

3 egg yolks
3/4 cup sugar
4 tablespoons cocoa
1 3/4 Valley Sanitary milk
4 tablespoons Pillsbury' s flour
1 teaspoon vanilla

Scald milk, mix sugar, cocoa and flour together. Add to milk and cook in double boiler until thick. Then add egg yolks and cook 5 minutes longer. Cool and pour into Graham cracker crust.

SOURCE: BROWNSVILLE HERALD, TEXAS, USA 1931

Black Bottom Pie III

Part 1
1 cup milk
4 tbsp cocoa or ground chocolate
1 1/4 tbsp cornstarch
3/4 cup sugar
1 tsp vanilla
1 tsp gelatine dissolved in 1 tsp. cold water.
Scald milk, mix dry ingredients, add to milk, cook in top of double
boiler 15 minutes, or until smooth. Remove, add gelatine and vanilla. When cold, fold in beaten whites of 2 eggs.

Part 2
1 tbsp gelatine
1/4 cup cold water
2 eggs
1/2 cup sugar
1/2 pint cream, whipped
Vanilla or rum flavouring
Soak gelatine, beat sugar with egg yolk, add milk, cook until cream.
Remove from the fire and add soaked gelatine and stir until cool.
When cold, fold in egg whites, beaten stiff. Cover top with whipped
cream sprinkled with grated chocolate or chocolate shot.

SOURCE: "KATHERINE PARSONS' COOKING COLUMN,"
VAN NUYS NEWS, CALIFORNIA, USA, 1932

Black Bottom Pudding

1/2 lb flour
1 tablespoonful currants
2 eggs
1 pint milk
1 dessertspoonful sugar
saltspoonful salt
1 teaspoonful baking powder

Grease a pudding mould, wash currants, and sprinkle in the bottom of it. Sift flour, salt and baking powder; break eggs into the middle; work round gradually, mixing in the flour; add milk steadily, and beat well. Pour into the prepared mould and steam 1 1/2 hours. Serve with sweet sauce.

SOURCE: THE DUBBO LIBERAL AND MACQUARIE ADVOCATE, 1907

Cock-a-Leekie

An old fowl, twelve leeks, half-a-pound of rice, two quarts of water, some pepper corns, and salt to taste. Pluck the fowl, draw, singe, and prepare it as for roasting. Next put it into a pot with the water and washed rice, the leeks cut in fine slices, and salt to taste.

Add the peppercorns, and cook all very gently for three hours. Then cut the meat from the fowl into small pieces, and serve it in the soup. The cooking of this soup must be very gentle, and if this meat is not tender at the end of the three hours allow more time. Scatter parsley over just before serving.

SOURCE: THE QUEENSLANDER, 1905

Cock-a-Leekie II

Boil an old fowl for three hours along with a good mutton bone; boil in the liquor for two hours the thick part of eight or ten leeks cut in pieces about one inch long; add twelve stoned prunes; boil for a quarter of an hour and serve piping hot.

SOURCE: WESTERN MAIL, PERTH, WA 1929

Cream Horns

Roll puff paste in a long rectangular piece, one-eighth inch thick. Cut in strips three-fourths inch wide. Roll paste over wooden forms bought for the purpose, having edges overlap. Bake in hot oven until well puffed and slightly browned. Brush over with white of egg slightly beaten, diluted with one teaspoon water, then sprinkle with sugar. Return to oven and finish cooking, and remove from forms. When cold, fill with Cream Filling or whipped cream sweetened and flavoured.

SOURCE: FARMER 1918

Dorset Knobs

About Dorset Knobs

The traditional recipe for Dorset Knobs is a closely guarded secret. It originated during the 1860s, in a bakery in Dorset, UK, after some leftover bread rolls dried out overnight in the cooling ovens. Samuel and Eleanor Moores, the bakers, realised they had stumbled upon a way of making bread remain edible for weeks, and began producing these hard, crisp, golden rounds, naming them after the locally crafted embroidered buttons.

Dorset Knobs' prolonged keeping qualities made them popular with the farming families in the district. People would eat them dunked in hot sweet tea and or put them in a bowl pour milk over, to make them soft.

To this day, Dorset Knobs are still made, from January to March, at Moores' Biscuit Bakery. The recipe has not changed much in 150 years. It is said that it takes three separate bakings to give the Knobs their crisp texture and unusual flavour, a process that takes about several hours.

We cannot know the original recipe, but after some intensive sleuthing, we have discovered one that is, if not identical, at least similar.

2 cups lukewarm water
4 tbsp sugar
1 scant tbsp yeast
4 tbsp butter
6 cups plain flour
2 tsp salt

Combine the lukewarm water and sugar and stir until the sugar dissolves completely

Sprinkle the yeast on top of the sugar-water. Do not stir it.

After about ten minutes, the yeast will froth a little and give off a pleasant smell.

Add the salt, butter, and three cups of the flour.

Mix until the ingredients come together to form a single mass.

Add another 2 1/2 cups of flour, and mix it in to form the dough. Sprinkle the other half cup of flour onto your kneading surface, then turn out the dough and knead it with your hands for three or four minutes.

Add the extra half cup of flour a little at a time, until you get a smooth and elastic dough. If it still feels sticky and wet after a few minutes, you can add a little extra flour.

When the dough has become springy and all sticks together, cease kneading.

Let the dough stand for a few minutes. Meanwhile, clean and grease the bowl you used for mixing. Place the dough in there, and cover with plastic wrap. Leave it in a warm place to rise for 1 to 1 1/2 hours. When the dough has doubled in size, gently punch it down and knead out any bubbles.

Divide it into chunks no bigger than golf balls and and place each piece about 2 cm apart on a lightly greased tray. Set the trays in a warm place and allow the dough to rise a second time, until the volume of the balls has doubled. This will take between 45 minutes and one hour.

While the bread is 'proving', preheat the oven to 180 C.

When the knobs have reached full size, put them in the oven and bake until golden brown. Once the baking is completed, turn the oven off, but leave the rolls in the cooling oven overnight until they dry out completely and become light and crisp.

Serve with Dorset Blue Vinney cheese and a tankard of old Dorset ale. Dorset Knobs can be split and buttered (though it is not easy to manage this, as they often break when sliced), or dunk them in a cup of tea with a teaspoon.

More About Dorset Knobs

'A Dorset Knob is a hard dry savoury biscuit which is today made by only a single producer, Moores Biscuits, in Morcombelake four miles west of Bridport in the west of the county of Dorset in England.

'Dorset Knobs are made from bread dough which contains extra sugar and butter. They are rolled and shaped by hand. They are baked three times. Once cooked, they are very crumbly and rather like very dry stale bread or rusks in consistency. They are named after Dorset knob buttons.

'Dorset Knobs are typically eaten with cheese (for example, Dorset Blue Vinney). They are normally sold in a distinctive and traditional tin. Dorset Knobs are said to have been a favourite food of local author Thomas Hardy.

'In the past there were a number of producers of Dorset Knobs. Today the only firm to produce them commercially is Moores Biscuits. The Moore family have baked biscuits in Dorset since before 1860. The bakery was established in 1880 by Samuel Moore and manufactures a variety of traditional biscuits in addition to the Dorset Knob. Dorset Knobs are only produced during the months of January and February. A Dorset Knob throwing competition is held in the Dorset village of Cattistock every year on the first Sunday in May.[3] The festival also includes such events as a knob and spoon race, knob darts, knob painting and guess the weight of the knob.'

SOURCE: WIKIPEDIA

Fitless Cock (Also called dry goose)

To make Fitless Cock mix together oatmeal, shredded suet and a finely chopped onion with a beaten egg.
Form into the shape of a chicken, wrap in cloth and boil for two hours.

2 cups oatmeal,
1 cup shredded suet and
1 cup finely chopped onion
1 -2 beaten eggs

Combine all ingredients. Shape in the form of a chicken, wrapped in a floured cloth and boil for two hours.

SOURCE: ANON

Note: During the war years of the 1940s the British Ministry of Food ran free cookery demonstrations. They advised economical cooks to try this meatless chicken-shaped oatmeal pudding, a traditional Scottish dish.

Gingernuts

One pound flour,
½lb treacle,
4oz butter,
½oz ginger,
1 teaspoonful soda,
3oz sugar,
Half-gill milk.

Put the flour, ginger, and sugar into a basin with a pinch of salt. Put the treacle and butter into a saucepan to melt; when it is quite warm add the milk.

Pour this upon the dry ingredients, and make into a firm paste; lightly flour the board, and turn it out; knead for a few minutes; then take small pieces and roll them into balls about the size of a walnut.

Put them on a buttered tin, and bake in a quick oven for five minutes.

SOURCE: THE SYDNEY MORNING HERALD, 1906

Jellyroll (Also known as Jam Roll)

Three eggs, the weight of three eggs in sugar, the weight of two in flour, one teaspoonful of cream tartar, half a teaspoonful of carbonate of soda; mix for about five minutes, put in a dish with buttered paper, and bake in a quick oven; spread with jam and roll.

SOURCE: SUNDAY TIMES, PERTH, WA 1905

Kisses

Take two eggs, a quarter pound of butter, half a pound of sugar, a quarter cup of milk, half a cup of cornflower [sic], a teaspoon of baking powder, and enough flour to make a stiff dough. Beat the eggs, butter, and sugar together. Add the cornflower [sic] and the milk, and finally the flour, with the baking powder. Drop in teaspoonsful on a well-greased slide. Bake in a brisk oven until a pale brown. Stick together in pairs with jam.

SOURCE: TOWNSVILLE DAILY BULLETIN, 1927

Ladies' Kisses I (Baci di dama)

70 g rice flour
70 g ground hazelnuts or ground almonds
50 g butter, softened
50 g brown sugar
30 g dark cooking chocolate
Pinch of salt

Preheat the oven to 160°C.

In a bowl, combine all the ingredients except the chocolate, and mix well. Make the mixture into a large ball, cover and chill in the refrigerator for 2 hours.

Form 30 small balls by gently rolling the dough between the palms of your hands. lace them 2 cm apart on a lightly buttered biscuit tray and bake in the oven for 15 minutes. Let them cool on the tray before removing.

Melt the chocolate over simmering water in a double saucepan. Spread a small dollop on the flat side of one biscuit and join a second biscuit to it with the chocolate 'glue'.

Leave the biscuits to allow the chocolate set before serving.

SOURCE: ANON

Note: Lady's Kisses are sweets originating in Piedmont in the Italian city of Tortona where they were first created a century ago. They are so called because they are formed from two cups of dough reminiscent of two pouting lips intending to kiss.

SOURCE: WIKIPEDIA

Ladies' Kisses II (Baci di dama)

100 grams of hazelnuts
100 grams of sugar
100 grams of butter, softened
Block of dark chocolate
100 grams of 00 flour ('Double zero' flour is the most-finely ground Italian durum wheat flour you can buy. "00" flour has a higher gluten content than plain flour and makes a more elastic dough. If it's unavailable, substitute plain flour.)

Toast the hazelnuts in the oven then, when ready, allow to cool, place in a mortar and grind to a powder.
Stir by hand all the ingredients until they are well blended. Don't worry about a few lumps.
Put the dough to rest in the fridge for an hour to become firm.
Shape into balls about 2 cm in diameter. Place on greased oven tray and bake at 150 degrees for about 15-20 minutes.
The secret of these biscuits is their cooking. The oven should be pre-heated but they should be cooked at a low temperature or when they come out they will be soft and difficult to handle. Overcooking makes their colour too dark and the flavor changes completely. Let them cool completely avoid breakage.
Meanwhile melt the chocolate in a double saucepan (without butter) and then, once the "shells" are cold, dip the flat side one at a time into the chocolate and join it to the flat side of another biscuit.
Place on a plate or on a tray ensuring that they stick together firmly then sprinkle with icing sugar and serve.

SOURCE: ANON

Note: You can use half hazelnuts and half almonds for a tastier result but the original recipe does NOT include use of almonds.
Kisses will last a week if stored in an airtight plastic container. If left in the open air they tend to soften and the chocolate melts.

Nipples of Venus I (Capezzoli di Venere)

Filling
225 g dark chocolate (70 per cent cocoa)
300 ml double cream

Covering
100 g dark chocolate (70 per cent cocoa)
50 g white chocolate

Filling: break the chocolate into small pieces and place in the top of a double saucepan. Melt the chocolate over simmering water.
Heat (do not boil) the cream in a small saucepan and add it to the melted chocolate, stirring until evenly blended.
Leave to cool for 2 hours.
When cool, use an electric machine to beat until the mixture becomes stiff and holds its shape.
Line 3 baking trays with baking paper. Put the filling mixture into a piping bag with a 1 cm plain nozzle and pipe little mounds -- or breasts -- on to the baking parchment.
Place in the fridge to chill and set.
Melt the dark chocolate in the double saucepan. Take each chilled breast and dip in the melted dark chocolate. Return to the parchment paper, place in refrigerator and allow it to set for an hour.
Melt the white chocolate in the double saucepan. Take each dark-chocolate-covered breast and dip the tip into the white chocolate to form a 'nipple'. Allow to set.

SOURCE ANON

Nipples of Venus II (Capezzoli di Venere)

With fresh chestnuts, the truffles are richer-tasting than with canned. For variety, add finely chopped toasted almonds or freshly-grated nutmeg to the truffle mixture."

Filling
6 oz bittersweet or semi-sweet chocolate
16 oz can whole chestnuts, or 1 1/4 pound fresh (fresh is best)
6 tablespoons butter
1/2 cup sugar
2 1/2 tablespoons brandy or other liqueur
1 teaspoon vanilla essence

Chocolate coating:
14 oz semi-sweet chocolate
1 to 1 1/2 cups pure cocoa powder

To prepare filling, melt chocolate in a double boiler and allow to cool. If using fresh chestnuts, cut a cross on the flat side of each shell, put in a large pan, cover with cold water, and boil for 5 minutes. Remove the shells and inner skins. Rinse the chestnuts.
Cream the butter and sugar together until fluffy, about 3 minutes. Add chestnuts and flavorings to the butter/sugar mixture and blend well, until chestnuts are mashed, then stir in the cooled chocolate. Mix well.
Cover and chill in the refrigerator for half an hour.
Roll into balls 1-1/2 inches in diameter and place on waxed paper on a greased tray. Chill.
To coat, melt the chocolate in a double saucepan over simmering water; allow to cool. Gently roll the truffle balls in melted chocolate, then place on a plate dusted with cocoa powder and allow to dry for several minutes. Dust each truffle with cocoa powder and place in paper candy cup. Store in an airtight container in the refrigerator.

SOURCE: ANON

About Nipples of Venus

Nipples of Venus *(Capezzoli di Venere)* are confections that featured in the 1984 film 'Amadeus' and were reputed to be enjoyed by Mozart's rival, Salieri.

In the movie 'Chocolat', Juliette Binoche's character 'Vianne Rocher' made Nipples of Venus to tempt the reserved and strait-laced Comte de Reynaud.

Since Mozart's days, this old recipe has been revived. Filled with chestnut and nougat paste they're enrobed in dark chocolate and resemble breasts topped with a nipple of white chocolate.

In some variations, these classic Italian truffles have a buttery chocolate and chestnut filling flavored with brandy.

Some cooks lightly tint the white chocolate with powdered (not liquid) red food colouring for pink 'nipples'

Nut Balls - Sweet

1 cup butter, softened
1/2 cup icing sugar
1/2 teaspoon salt
1 teaspoon almond essence
2 cups plain flour
1 1/2 cups finely chopped walnuts
Castor sugar

Beat butter with sugar until creamy. Add salt, almond or vanilla, flour, and nuts. Mix thoroughly. Chill dough until firm enough to handle.
Preheat oven to 180 degrees C (350 degrees F). Shape dough into 2 cm balls. Place on ungreased biscuit tray. Bake for 12 to 15 minutes or until light brown. While balls are still warm, roll in castor sugar.

SOURCE: ANON

Nut Balls - Savoury

Take about 1 1b. of cold cooked potato, 1 tablespoon of chopped parsley, salt and pepper, a few almonds, a little chopped onion, 2oz. of butter, some chopped nuts.
Mash the potato and heat it in a saucepan with the butter, chopped parsley, onion, and seasoning, adding a little milk if necessary.
Beat it until it is quite smooth, then shape it into neat balls.
Make a hole in the centre of each ball and fill it in with mixed, chopped nuts. Slightly grease a fireproof dish, put the potato balls in it, and stick into each some of the blanched and shredded almonds.
Cook them in a moderate oven for about a quarter of an hour. Serve them very hot, and, if possible, with some savoury sauce.

SOURCE: EXAMINER, LAUNCESTON, TAS. 1933

Pricked Beef (Casne pinchada)

1 kg beef for roasting
1 large green capsicum, finely chopped
1 large onion, finely chopped
Garlic powder
Salt and pepper
350 ml tea sweetened with molasses
Vanilla essence
Prunes (optional)

Prick beef with knife. Stuff the holes with onions and green pepper, also prunes if desired.
Sprinkle garlic powder, salt and pepper, and pour the sweetened tea over the beef. Place it in the oven at 180 degrees C (350 degrees F). Roast for approximately 1 hour.

SOURCE: ANON

Red Lips
(Traditional Swedish cookies)

1 cup butter, softened
1/2 cup sugar
2 cups flour
3/4 cup raspberry jam

Preheat oven to 190C (375F)
In a medium bowl, beat butter 30 seconds.
Beat in sugar until combined.
Beat in as much flour as you can.
Stir in any remaining flour.
Shape dough into 2.5 cm diameter balls.
Place balls 5 cm apart on an un-greased biscuit tray.
Press your thumb into the centre of each ball to make a dent.
Bake for about 12 minutes or until edges are lightly browned.
Transfer cookies to a wire rack to cool.
Just before serving, fill each centre with about 1 tsp of jam.

SOURCE: ANON

Spotted Dick I

Cream two-thirds cup sugar and 1 heaped tablespoon dripping together. Work into this 2 heaped cups flour, to which has been added 1 teaspoon soda and 2 cream of tartar, pinch salt, add 1/2 cup currants, 1/2 cup sultanas, then add to mixture sufficient milk and water to make dough quite wet, or just too wet to be handled. Have ready dry pudding cloth on which is placed greased paper. Spoon the mixture on to paper in roll form, roll up in paper, then cloth, and tie; boil for one hour and a half.

SOURCE: THE CENTRAL QUEENSLAND HERALD, 1939

Spotted Dick II

Mix together 1/2 lb. flour, a pinch of salt, 3 oz. suet, add 1 tea-spoon baking powder and 2 tablespoons sugar.
Wash and dry 2 oz. currants or sultanas, and stir these into the mixture. Make a stiff dough with cold water or milk.
Form into a roll, tie in a scalded and well-floured cloth, and boil for 2 1/4 hours.
Serve with jam sauce or custard (boiled milk is just as nice). This is a very substantial and economical pudding.

SOURCE: THE CENTRAL QUEENSLAND HERALD, 1942
'"Silver Tide" comes second with this spotted dick pudding.'

11
SNOW

Apple Snow

Take 1 lb. apples, 1/4lb. sugar, whites of 3 eggs, add a packet of lemon jelly crystals.
Peel and core the apples, cooking with very little water till tender. Beat fine, and when cool add the beaten whites of eggs and sugar. Whip till snowy and thick. Having made and set the jelly, ornament the dish with lumps of it.

SOURCE: THE DAILY NEWS, PERTH, WA 1919

Moulded Snow

4 cups scalded milk
1/4 teaspoon salt
1/2 cup corn-starch
1/2 cup cold milk
1/4 cup sugar
1 teaspoon vanilla
Whites 3 eggs

Mix corn-starch, sugar, and salt, dilute with cold milk, add to scalded milk, stirring constantly until mixture thickens, afterwards occasionally; cook fifteen minutes.
Add flavouring and whites of eggs beaten stiff, mix thoroughly, mould, chill, and serve with serve with Chocolate Ice.

SOURCE: FARMER, 1918

Snowballs

1/2 cup butter
2 1/4 cups flour
1 cup sugar
3 1/2 teaspoons baking powder
1/2 cup milk
Whites 4 eggs

Cream the butter, add sugar gradually, milk, and flour mixed and sifted with baking powder; then add the whites of eggs beaten stiff. Steam thirty-five minutes in buttered cups; serve with preserved fruit, quince marmalade, or strawberry sauce.

SOURCE: FARMER, 1918

Snow Cake

1/4 cup butter
2 1/2 teaspoons baking powder
1 cup sugar
Whites 2 eggs
1/2 cup milk
1/2 teaspoon vanilla or
1 2/3 cups flour
1/4 teaspoon almond extract

Follow recipe for mixing butter cakes. To Mix Butter Cakes. An earthen bowl should always be used for mixing cake, and a wooden cake-spoon with slits lightens the labor. Measure dry ingredients, and mix and sift baking powder and spices, if used, with flour.

Count out number of eggs required, breaking each separately that there may be no loss should a stale egg chance to be found in the number, separating yolks from whites if rule so specifies.

Measure butter, then liquid. Having everything in readiness, the mixing may be quickly accomplished. If butter is very hard, by allowing it to stand a short time in a warm room it is measured and creamed much easier. If time cannot be allowed for this to be done, warm bowl by pouring in some hot water, letting stand one minute, then emptying and wiping dry.

Avoid overheating bowl, as butter will become oily rather than creamy.

Put butter in bowl, and cream by working with a wooden spoon until soft and of a creamy consistency; then add sugar gradually, and continue beating.

Add yolks of eggs or whole eggs beaten until light, liquid, and flour mixed and sifted with baking powder; or liquid and flour may be added alternately. When yolks and whites of eggs are beaten separately, whites are usually added at the last, as is the case when whites of eggs alone are used.

A cake can be made fine-grained only by long beating, although light and delicate with a small amount of beating. Never stir cake after the final beating, remembering that beating motion should always be the last used. Bake Snow Cake forty-five minutes in a deep narrow pan.

SOURCE: FARMER, 1918

Snow Eggs I

Put 1 1/2 pint of milk into a lined stewpan with the rind of a lemon and sufficient castor sugar to sweeten nicely. Let this stand on a moderate heat for about half an hour, then remove the peel.

Take the whites of eight eggs, and whisk to a very stiff froth, that is to say, until it is a perfectly solid mass.

Bring the milk to boiling point, and then proceed to drop in the egg froth in tablespoonfuls, turning them gently round until they seem cooked. Then carefully remove and place in a glass dish. Meanwhile beat up the yolk of the eggs, add to them tho milk and stir one way carefully until the custard is made. Pour this round the eggs and put aside until perfectly cold.

SOURCE: THE SYDNEY MORNING HERALD, 1906

Snow Eggs and Stewed Fruit

This is a delicious dish for hot weather.

Divide the whites from the yolks of three eggs and whisk the former to a very stiff froth with a teaspoonful of castor sugar.

Put rather more than a pint of milk, sweetened, to taste, in a stewpan, and when it boils drop in the white of an egg in dessertspoonfuls.

Poach each spoonful for about Five minutes, and when cooked lift them out with an egg slice, and put on a sieve to drain. When all the white of an egg has been used, strain the milk, and add it to the beaten yolks, with a few drops of essence of lemon.

Pour back again, to the stewpan, and add a teaspoonful of flour moistened with a little cold milk. Stir over the fire until the custard begins to thicken (but not boil).

When cold, pour into a glass dish, and lay the snow eggs on the top. Serve with any kind of fresh stewed fruit cooked in the ordinary manner, and biscuits.

Raspberries or red currants make a charming and refreshing accompaniment on account of their flavour and colour.

SOURCE: MORNING BULLETIN, QLD 1905

Snowflake Cake

Take a half-cupful of butter, three eggs, two cupfuls of
sugar, four of flour, one of milk, tAVO teaspoonfuls of Royal
Baking Powder. Stir butter and sugar together, add the
beaten yolks and half the flour, with the baking powder in it;
pour in the milk, beat the whites and mix in ; then stir in the
rest of the flour. Bake in jelly-cake tins. Grate two cocoanuts,
add to them one cup of sugar and the beaten whites of
two eggs ; spread between the cakes, and heap the cocoanut
on top.

SOURCE: HOWSON, 1881

Snow Pudding I

1/4 box gelatine or
1 cup boiling water
1 tablespoon granulated gelatine
1 cup sugar
1/4 cup cold water
1/4 cup lemon juice
Whites 3 eggs

Soak gelatine in cold water, dissolve in boiling water, add sugar
and lemon juice, strain, and set aside in cool place; occasionally stir
mixture, and when quite thick, beat with wire spoon or whisk until
frothy; add whites of eggs beaten stiff, and continue beating until
stiff enough to hold its shape. Mould, or pile by spoonfuls on glass
dish; serve cold with Boiled Custard. A very attractive dish may be
prepared by coloring half the mixture with fruit red.

SOURCE: FARMER, 1918

Snow Pudding II

Beat whites of four eggs until stiff, add one-half tablespoon granulated gelatine dissolved in three tablespoons boiling water, beat until thoroughly mixed, add one-fourth cup powdered sugar, and flavor with one-half teaspoon lemon extract. Pile lightly on dish, serve with Boiled Custard.

SOURCE: FARMER, 1918

Snow Pudding III

Put some water on some gelatine and let it stand ; then take the whites of eggs and beat light ; then add them to the gala tine; beat well; then put it in a form. Eat with a sauce of soft custard, flavored with lemon.

SOURCE: HOWSON, 1881

White Christmas

250 g Copha or white chocolate
1 cup (100 g) milk powder
1 cup (30 g) rice bubbles
1 cup (175 g) Mixed dried and glace fruit and glace citrus peel
1 cup (150 g) icing sugar
1 cup (90 g) desiccated coconut

Melt Copha or white chocolate over gentle heat. Combine remaining ingredients together. Pour melted Copha or white chocolate over the mixture and stir well. Press into a greased tray and chill until firm. Cut into squares.

The mixture could also be spooned into small paper cupcake cases for children, or the squares can be wrapped in cellophane and given as Christmas presents.

SOURCE: ANON

About White Christmas

White Christmas is an Australian sweet treat. It is a popular Christmas food item, especially as it can easily be made by children. The mixture of dried and glace fruits and crystallized citrus rinds echoes the ingredients of a traditional Christmas pudding, while the hydrogenated coconut oil (Copha) or white chocolate surrounds the colourful fruits with a snowy hue. 'White Christmas' refers to the presence of snow on Christmas Day in the Northern Hemisphere. (It is also the title of a song and a movie.) In Australia Christmas Day falls in the hot summer, so they replace the snow of a White Christmas with this rich snack.

SOURCE: WIKIPEDIA

12

SPOOKY

Black Midnight Cake

Betty Crocker published a recipe for Black Midnight Cake, but her work is still in copyright, and we will not reproduce it here.
Her recipe, however, is similar to a Chocolate Cake recipe in the The Sydney Morning Herald of August 1950.

1 cup S R flour
3/4 cup sugar
2 dspns cocoa
1 tbspn melted butter
1/2 cup milk
1 egg (unbeaten)
Vanilla essence

Place all ingredients in basin in above order, and mix for two minutes. Pour into a greased sandwich or bar tin and bake for 1 hr. in a moderate oven. Ice with chocolate icing when cool.

Chocolate Icing
Mix together 1/2 cup icing sugar, 1/2 tspn. cocoa and 1 large tspn. butter, blended with 1 dspn. boiling water. Warm them on the stove then spread on cake.

SOURCE: THE SYDNEY MORNING HERALD 1950
'THIS week's prize of £3/3/ for "The Recipe of the Week" goes to MISS BERNA LAWSON, 17 Lindsay Avenue, Yarra Bay'

Bones of the Dead (Ossi dei Morti)

1/4 cup fine semolina flour
2 tablespoons fine semolina flour
2 large egg whites, at room temperature
2/3 cup icing sugar
2/3 cup coarsely chopped cooking chocolate
3/4 cup coarsely chopped blanched almonds

Icing
2/3 cup coarsely chopped cooking chocolate
2 tablespoons butter

Preheat oven to 150°C (300°F). Lavishly grease baking trays and sprinkle them with flour, or line them with baking paper.

In a copper or glass bowl, whip the egg whites until stiff peaks start to form. Gradually add half the sugar a little at a time, beating until well mixed and the whites are stiff and shiny. Sprinkle the remaining sugar, semolina flour, chocolate, and almonds over the egg whites and fold in with a rubber spatula.

Using a pair of teaspoons as tongs, shape a small piece of batter into bone-shaped biscuits about 7cm (3 inches) long and 4cm (1½ inches) wide.

If you wish, you can make a cardboard template in the shape of a bone and trace the outline with a pencil onto the underside of the parchment paper, then fill in the shape with the batter.

Space the biscuits about 2.5 cm (1 inch) apart.

Bake for 30 to 35 minutes or until the biscuits are quite dry but have not started to go brown. Cool them on the trays, then transfer them gently to a wire rack.

(Continued next page)

Icing: Fill the bottom of a double saucepan with water and bring to a boil. Turn off the heat, add the chocolate and butter to the top saucepan, put on the lid and allow the mixture to stand for 10 to 15 minutes until the chocolate and butter have melted.

Stir the icing well. Dip the underside of each biscuit into it and, before it has set, draw wavy lines through the chocolate with a fork. Allow the biscuits to dry completely.

SOURCE: ANON

About Bones of the Dead

Ossi dei morti ("bones of the dead") biscuits are a popular treat in Italy on All Saints Day. This day is sometimes called the Day of the Dead, but it is far from being a mournful occasion.

Instead it is a celebration, in loving memory of family members who have passed away. Ossi dei Morti are named not only for the day on which they are enjoyed, but also because of their shape, pallor and texture. Traditional ossi dei morti usually consist of hard meringue that, when eaten, crunches like dry bones.

Every Italian region has its own variation on the recipe for these delicious treats. Some add cinnamon, cloves and citrus zest.

Dead Man over Worms (Meatloaf over Spaghetti Noodles)

Meat Loaf
One cup meat, put through chopper,
1 tablespoon minced parsley,
1/2 teaspoon salt,
1/2 teaspoon pepper,
1 tablespoon poultry seasoning,
1/2 cup bread crumbs.

Mix left-over meat that has been chopped, adding to it the Ingredients in the order given. Mix well and moisten with beef or chicken gravy. Form in a loaf of the desired shape. Bake thirty minutes. Serve hot with tomato sauce or cold for lunches.

SOURCE: TOWNSVILLE DAILY BULLETIN, 1922

Noodles
Beat two eggs slightly; add two tablespoonfuls of milk and half a teaspoonful of salt. Stir in flour enough to make a very stiff dough. Knead it till stiff as possible.

Roll it out into rectangular pieces and so thin you can see through it. Lay them on a napkin half an hour until they are dry, but not brittle. Rub over with a little flour so it will not stick.

Roll up tight and hard and then slice off from the end about one-eighth of an inch thick. Shake them out till long and straight.

Put them into boiling salted water, stir them at first to prevent sticking and cook until they swell and come to the top of the water. Skim them out into a dish for serving.

SOURCE: THE CUMBERLAND ARGUS AND FRUITGROWERS ADVOCATE ,1895

(Continued next page)

Sauce

1 cup tomato ketchup
1 cup packed brown sugar dissolved in 1/2 cup boiling water
2 teaspoon prepared mustard
1 teaspoon butter

To Assemble the Dish: Put noodles on dish, place meatloaf on top of spaghetti noodles. Pour sauce over the top.

Dead Man's Leg
(Also known as Jam Roly-Poly Pudding)

For the suet crust, to every pound of flour allow 5 or 6 oz. of beef suet, 1/2 pint of water.

Free the suet from skin and shreds; chop it extremely fine, and rub it well into the flour; work the whole to a smooth paste with the above proportion of water; roll it out, and it is ready for use. This crust is quite rich enough for ordinary purposes, but when a better one is desired, use from 1/2 to 3/4 lb. of suet to every lb. of flour. Some cooks, for rich crusts, pound the suet in a mortar, with a small quantity of butter. It should then be laid on the paste in small pieces, the same as for puff-crust, and will be found exceedingly nice for hot tarts. 5 oz. of suet to every lb. of flour will make a very good crust; and even 1/4 lb. will answer very well for children, or where the crust is wanted very plain.

Roll out 3/4 lb suet crust to the thickness of about 1/2 inch. Spread 3/4 lb. of any kind of jam [preferably raspberry or strawberry] equally over it, leaving a small margin of paste without any, where the pudding joins.

Roll it up, fasten the ends securely, and tie it in a floured cloth; put the pudding into boiling water, and boil for 2 hours.

Time 2 hours.
Average cost 9d.
Sufficient for 5 or 6 persons.

SOURCE: MRS BEETON 1861

Notes on Dead Man's Leg

Jam Roly-Poly, Dead Man's Arm or Dead Man's Leg is a tradi-tional British dessert probably invented in the early 19th century. It is a flat-rolled suet pudding, which is then spread with jam and rolled up, similar to a Swiss roll.

In days past, Jam Roly-Poly was also known as shirt-sleeve pudding, because it was often steamed and served in an old shirt-sleeve. Because of this, [and because the red jam against the pale pudding resembled blood], another nickname for the pudding was dead-man's arm, or dead man's leg.

Jam Roly-Poly features in Mrs Beeton's cookery book, as Roly-Poly Jam Pudding. This pudding is one of a range of pud-dings that are now considered classic desserts of mid 20th century British school dinners.

SOURCE: WIKIPEDIA

Death by Chocolate

Ingredients for cake
8 oz (225 g) dark semisweet chocolate (40-50% cocoa)
2/3 cup (140 g) butter
1 cup (210 g) sugar
4 eggs
4 heaped tablespoons (10 ml) plain flour
4 tablespoons unsweetened cocoa powder
1½ teaspoon baking powder or 1 teaspoon baking soda
1 teaspoon vanilla essence
4 tablespoons sour cream

Ingredients for icing
2/3 cup (160 ml) heavy cream or whipping cream
9 oz (260 g) semisweet chocolate (40-50% cocoa)

Preheat oven to 350 deg F (Gas mark 4 or 180 deg C). Line a circular 10 inch (25 cm) cake tin 3 inches (8cm) high with grease proof or other non-stick paper and grease the tin. The cake will rise to 8 cm and collapse a little when cool. If your cake tin is less than 25 cm in diameter and 8 cm tall it is best to use two cake tins.
Break the chocolate into small pieces and melt it with butter in a double saucepan over hot water.
Beat the eggs with sugar, mix with flour, cocoa powder, baking powder and vanilla essence.
Slowly fold in the melted butter and chocolate and the sour cream. Bake at 180C (350F) degrees until a skewer inserted in centre comes out clean, approximately 40 to 50 minutes (if using 2 cake tins 20-30 minutes may be sufficient).
Cool the cake completely. When it has reached room temperature, place it in the refrigerator for at least 30 minutes before removing the cake from the tin (the cake is sticky and difficult to cut when it is warm!)

Remove the crusted surface on the top of the cake, and cut in half, horizontally. (Continued next page)

Icing:

Heat 2/3 cup (160 ml) of heavy cream or whipping cream in a saucepan.

Remove from heat, add 9 oz (260 g) of finely chopped dark semi-sweet chocolate, stir until smooth, and let it cool until in thickens.

Use one 1/3 of the frosting between the two layers, 1/3 on top, and the rest around the cake. Put the cake into the fridge for one hour or more to harden the frosting.

This cake should be served at room temperature.

Variations

Add 3 tablespoons of rum to the chocolate and butter mixture.
Add chopped walnuts and decorate with whole walnuts.

SOURCE: ANON

About Death by Chocolate

Death by Chocolate is a marketing term for various desserts that feature chocolate (especially dark chocolate or cocoa) as the primary ingredient. The trademark in the United States was owned by S&A Restaurant Group, the parent company of Bennigan's restaurants, but with the subsequent bankruptcy of the company the current legal status is unclear. In the United Kingdom and European Union, the registered trade mark rights belong to F.T. Wood & Sons Limited. Nevertheless, unlicensed uses of the term are common.

In the late 1970s, several restaurants in the Cleveland, Ohio, area offered a "Death by Chocolate" dessert in response to the demand created by the mention of a fictional dish of the same name on Linn Sheldon's Barnaby & Friends children's television show. This usually consisted of chocolate cake, chocolate ice cream, chocolate brownies and chocolate syrup layered in a tall parfait glass.

In 1981 Jeffrey Fields opened a restaurant in Los Angeles called Les Anges. He and his French Pastry Chef invented a chocolate cake that they called "La Mort au Chocolat", translated as "Death by Chocolate" and "Chocolate Death". It was on the menu on opening day and remained very popular throughout the life of the restaurant. The original Les Anges creation included multiple layers of chocolate genoise, mousse, ganache, and meringue. It was dressed with chocolate crème anglaise.

Reference to the dessert first appeared in a Los Angeles Times review, by critic Lois Dwan, on 13 September 1981.

A dish called "Death by Chocolate" might be -

A layered chocolate cake, with fudge, ganache, or chocolate mousse between the layers

A dessert made in a trifle bowl from alternating layers of broken-up Kahlúa-soaked brownies, chocolate mousse, crushed Heath bars, and whipped topping

A molten chocolate cake

A flourless chocolate cake (sometimes called "chocolate decadence")

SOURCE: WIKIPEDIA

Magic Biscuits

3 cups of flour
2 teaspoons cream of tartar
1 teaspoon of soda
1/2 teaspoon of salt,
2 heaping tablespoons of shortening.

'Sieve the flour, cream of tartar and salt into a bowl and rub in the shortening, taking care that my hands are very cool.
I dissolve the soda in the first cup of milk and water, as it usually takes part of a second cup for the quantity of flour.
The dough, though soft, should be stiff to be lifted easily on to the baking board, the latter being well sprinkled with flour.
Do not roll out, but pat with well-floured fingers until it is about half an inch thick; then cut into rounds with a cutter, or into squares with a well-floured knife.
If these biscuits are fried in boiling lard like doughnuts, opened with a fork and filled with jam or stewed fruit, they are unbelievably good.
This recipe serves for fruit shortcake or mock meat pie. If baked in layer cake tins it may also be used for hot pies, or if a little more milk is added, dropped into gem pans it makes delicious muffins.'

SOURCE: SUNDAY TIMES, PERTH, WA 1932
'My recipe for delicious flaky hot biscuits.'

Magic Mayonnaise

Take 1 cup vinegar, 1/4 cup salad oil or melted butter, 1 egg yolk, 1/2 teaspoon salt, 1 teaspoon dry mustard, sprinkle of cayenne, two-thirds of a cup of condensed milk. Place ingredients in a jar, fasten top on tightly and shake well for two minutes. The mixture will blend perfectly. If thicker consistency is required place jar in refrigerator to chill before serving.

To double recipe: The recipe may be doubled by using 1 whole egg in place of the egg yolk, and doubling all other ingredients. This will make 2 1/2 cups mayonnaise.

SOURCE: SUNDAY TIMES, PERTH, WA 1933

Magic Butter

'For those who often make sandwiches for a supper dish, or contribute a few dozen for supper at social functions, here is a tip to make your precious butter go further. The recipe for "Magic Butter" was sent in by Mrs. M. Hawkins, 96 Invermay Rd., Launceston, and wins the Jean Nelson prize of 10/6 this week.'

1/2 lb. butter,
1/2 lb. margarine,
1 cup hot water (not boiling),
1 cup cold water,
1 teaspoon salt.

Put butter and margarine in mixing bowl and break in small pieces. Add salt, and gradually add first a little hot water then a little cold until all water is used up. Beat well until tho roughly blended.

Divide mixture into four. Leave one portion plain and use like butter. To the second portion add grated onion; to third, 1 dessertspoon peanut butter, and to last grated cheese or minced ham. Delicious for sandwiches.

SOURCE: EXAMINER, LAUNCESTON, TAS. 1951

Midnight Cake

6 oz butter
1 1/4 cups sugar
1 tblspn boiling water
3 eggs
2 1/2 cups S R flour. Good pinch salt
1/4 level tspn baking soda
3 level tblspns cocoa.
3/4 cup milk
4 tblspns boiling water

Cream butter and sugar with one tblspn boiling water. Add eggs one at a time, beating well after adding each one.
Blend cocoa with milk. Mix flour, soda, and salt. Add to creamed mixture alternately with milk and cocoa, adding boiling water. Divide between two 9in sandwich tins, spreading evenly. Bake in mod. oven until quite cooked, about 20 min.
When cool, split each layer, fill with chocolate filling, ice all over with warm icing.
Decorate with a humped backed Hallowe'en cat.

Hallowe'en Cat

Cream 2oz butter, add 1 level tblspn. cocoa, 1 tspn. coffee essence, 1 cup sifted icing sugar. Beat well.
Trace cat from nursery book. Cut out and use to outline cat on top of cake, carefully fill in with chocolate icing.
Put remaining icing in forcing bag with plain pipe attached, and pipe fence under cat.

SOURCE: THE SYDNEY MORNING HERALD 1954

Monster Cookies

4 1/2 cups quick-cooking rolled oats
1 cup light brown sugar
1 cup white sugar
1 1/2 cups peanut butter
8 tablespoons butter, softened
3 large eggs
1 tablespoon vanilla essence
2 teaspoons baking soda
1 cup semi-sweet chocolate chips
1 cup Smarties or other candy-coated chocolate buttons

Preheat oven to 180°C (350°F). Grease baking trays butter or oil, or line with baking paper.

In a large bowl, combine the peanut butter with the sugars and butter. Beat with an electric mixer until thoroughly blended. Add the eggs and vanilla. Beat in the oats and baking soda. Remove bowl from electric mixer and by hand, stir in the chocolate chips and coloured sweets, reserving some for last minute decorations.

Spoon large heaps of cookie doughs onto the prepared baking trays. Dot a few extra sweets and chocolate chips on top of each mound of dough before putting trays in the oven. Some people use an ice cream scoop instead of a spoon to ladle the dough onto the baking tray, which creates huge cookies.

Bake for 10 to 12 minutes for normal-sized cookies or 18 to 20 minutes for ice-cream scoop giant ones. Do not overcook or the colour will be too dark and the chocolate chips will lose their shape. Remove from oven and cool for 5 minutes on trays until cookies are firm. Transfer to wire racks and let them cool completely before storing in an airtight container.

SOURCE: ANON

About Monster Cookies

Monster cookies have been around since the 1940s when the Rowntree Chocolate Company started distributing its 'chocolate beans' - candy-covered buttons of milk chocolate which later became known as 'Smarties'.

The cookies, which are made of peanut butter and oatmeal mixed with chocolate chips and studded with colourful sweets, get their name from their generous size.

In turn, they lent their name to a character on the children's TV show 'Sesame Street'.

Witch Cake

Beat to a cream 4oz butter and 5 oz castor sugar; add the yolks of 2 eggs and the grated rind of an orange with a teaspoonful of the juice.
Sieve 1/2 lb flour and 2oz rice flour with a heaped teaspoonful baking powder and add.

Fold in whisked whites of eggs and a cupful of milk.
Bake in a hot oven for about 40 minutes and when cold shape the top to form a roof.

Cover with plain white icing flavoured with orange juice and when it is dry, indicate doors and windows with chocolate icing.

Make the chimneys with blobs of yellow marzipan and perch a witch on the roof.

(If preferred, vanilla can be used instead of orange for flavouring.)

> Source: The West Australian, October 1938
> 'HALLOWE'EN PARTY. Suggestions for a Festive Occasion. Here are some recipes which would fit in with the occasion. Have one cake in the form of a witch's cottage. If you make it in an oblong, rather high, biscuit tin, it will be the right shape, and the following recipe is appetising without being elaborate:'

13
YOU SAID WHAT?

Crullers

1/4 cup butter
4 cups flour
1 cup sugar
1/4 teaspoon grated nutmeg
Yolks 2 eggs
31/2 teaspoons baking powder
Whites 2 eggs
1 cup milk
Powdered sugar and cinnamon

Cream the butter, add sugar gradually, yolks of eggs well beaten, and whites of eggs beaten stiff. Mix flour, nutmeg, and baking powder; add alternately with milk to first mixture; toss on floured board, roll thin, and cut in pieces three inches long by two inches wide; make four one-inch parallel gashes crosswise at equal intervals. Take up by running finger in and out of gashes, and lower into deep fat to fry. After frying take up on a skewer, and drain on brown paper. Add trimmings to one-half remaining mixture, roll, shape, and fry as before; repeat. Doughnuts should come quickly to top of fat, brown on one side, then be turned to brown on the other; avoid turning more than once. The fat must be kept at a uniform temperature. If too cold, doughnuts will absorb fat; if too hot, doughnuts will brown before sufficiently risen. See rule for testing fat.

SOURCE: FARMER, 1918

Flummery I

Dissolve one ounce of gelatine in one pint of boiling water, and let it stand for two hours. Pour into a saucepan with a quarter of a pound of sugar , the juice and peel of a lemon, and the yolks of four eggs. Set the pan on the fire and stir the contents till it boils. Then strain through a flannel bag, and when almost cold pour into a mould.

SOURCE: THE CUMBERLAND ARGUS AND FRUITGROW-ERS ADVOCATE PARRAMATTA, NSW 1894
'Flummery is an old fashioned sweet that one seldom hears of now, so I was surprised at your wishing to make it. Here is an excellent recipe.'

Flummery II

Take 1 cup water, 1 cup sugar, large tablespoon gelatine, boiled together for about five minutes after boiling point is reached.
Then mix one tablespoon plain flour, with little cold water, and the juice of two lemons, two oranges or passion fruit, strained; add to boiling mixture; stand to cool, and beat well with egg.
Whisk for half an hour.
This is beautiful with any stewed fruit for dessert.

SOURCE: THE DAILY NEWS, PERTH, WA 1928

Flummery III

Take 1 oz of gelatine,
3 lemons,
6 oz sugar,
Yhe yolks of two eggs,
And a short pint of boiling water.

Soak the gelatine in cold water while you grate the rind of 1 lemon, and squeeze the juice of 3 over the sugar; dissolve the gelatine in the boiling water and add to it the lemon and sugar, stirring for a few moments with a silver or wooden spoon.
Then add the egg yolks and stir well till the egg is mixed.
Strain through muslin into a pot or glass mould. If you like, the whites of egg may be whisked and added to the jelly, when ready for setting, and the whole whisked till firm.

Source: The West Australian, 1936
'Flummery is delicious, as this old Yorkshire recipe will prove to you:'

About Flummery

Wikipedia says 'Flummery (Welsh: llymru) is a sweet soft pudding that is at present made from stewed fruit and thickened with cornstarch.

'Wales -

'Flummery was essentially a Welsh dish which subsequently entered the culinary repertoire of the English. It was first mentioned in 1620s, "a type of coagulated food" like sour oatmeal jelly boiled with the husks, or, as an acid preparation from the husks and fragments of oats, fermented and subacid oatmeal, its acridity and sharpness explaining the Welsh etymology of lym = sharp, similar to the Scotch sour sowens. Another improbable etymology sends to the German Pflaumerei (plum tarte), there is a variety of flummery called 'plum flummery'. The Welsh flummery is called llumruwd (sour sediment) and it is formed of the husks of the oatmeal roughly sifted out, soaked in water till it becomes sour, then strained and boiled, when it forms a pale brown sub-gelatinous mass, usually eaten with abundance of new milk. The true Welsh flummery is called in parts of Wales "sucan blawd" (steeped meal).

'Elsewhere in Britain -

'Traditional British flummeries were, like the Scottish porridges, often oatmeal-based and cooked to achieve a smooth and gelatinous texture; sugar and milk were typically added and occasionally orange flower water. The dish is typically bland in nature. The dish gained stature in the 17th century where it was prepared in elaborate molds and served with applause from the dining audience.

'The word also came to mean generally dishes made with milk, eggs and flour in the late seventeenth and during the nineteenth centuries. It later came to have more negative connotations as a bland, empty and unsatisfying food.

'In Australia and U.S. -

'In Australia, post World War II, flummery was known as a mousse dessert made with beaten evaporated milk, sugar and gelatine. Also made using jelly crystals, mousse flummery became established as an inexpensive alternative to traditional cream-based mousse in Australia. The writer Bill Bryson described flummery as an early form of blancmange.

'In Ireland -

'A pint of flummery was suggested as an alternative to 4 ounces (110 g) of bread and a 0.5 imperial pints (0.28 l) of new milk for the supper of sick inmates in Irish Workhouses in the 1840s.

'Figurative use -

'Flummery's negative connotation was picked up in its alternate, figurative meaning: empty compliments, unsubstantial talk or writing, and nonsense. The term is also used to denote intentionally confusing speech, flim-flam."

Fricassee

680 g rabbit, chicken, turkey or other white meat
1 teaspoon salt
1 onion
450 ml chicken stock or water
1/2 turnip
30 g flour (2 tablespoons)
2 pieces celery
30g butter (2 tablespoons)
6 peppercorns
150 ml milk
3 shakes of white pepper
Chopped parsley for garnish

Chop meat into small pieces. Put it into a saucepan with stock, salt and peppercorns and bring to the boil.Peel and cut up vegetables and add to saucepan. Place lid on saucepan and simmer until tender - approx. 1 1/2 hours. Remove from heat and skim the fat off the top. Take out the meat and vegetables. Put them on a serving dish and keep them hot.
Make white sauce using the butter, flour and milk, mixed with 300ml of the stock from the fricassee. Add pepper. Pour over the meat and vegetables on the serving dish, sprinkle with parsley. Serve with mashed potatoes or rice.

SOURCE: ANON

Notes about Fricassee
Wikipedia says "Fricassee ... is any stewed dish typically made with poultry, although other types of white meat can be substituted. It is cut into pieces and then stewed in gravy, which is then thickened with butter and cream or milk. It often includes other ingredients and vegetables."
"The Online Etymology Dictionary says that this word originated in the 1560s, from Middle French. At that time, 'fricassée' was the feminine past participle of 'fricasser', meaning 'to mince and cook in sauce.'"

Kedgeree

Salmon kedgeree may be served as an entree or with suitable vegetables, as the main course of a meal.

To prepare take: 1 lb. of salmon, 6oz. Rice, 2 hard-boiled eggs, 2oz. Butter, seasoning. Boil and dry the rice, flake the salmon and cut the eggs into slices.

Melt the butter in a stew pan, add to it the fish, rice, whites of eggs, salt, pepper and cayenne to taste and stir over a moderate heat until piping hot. Turn the mixture on to a hot dish, press into a pyramid form with a fork, decorate with the yolk of egg and serve at once.

SOURCE: THE WEST AUSTRALIAN, 1937

Rumtum Tiddy
(Also known as Rum Tum Ditty, Ring Tum Diddy)

230 g cheddar cheese, chopped
1 x 300 g can condensed tomato soup
1 teaspoon Worcestershire sauce
2 tablespoons finely diced onion
1/8 teaspoon pepper
4 slices bread, toasted
1 tablespoon chopped chives

Mix the cheese, tomato soup, Worcestershire sauce, onion and pepper in a saucepan.

Stir over medium heat until the cheese is completely melted.Remove the saucepan from the heat for a minute or two until the cheese mixture becomes a little firmer. Pour mixture onto the slices of toast and grill until the tops start to bubble -- but don't let them brown.

Sprinkle with chives to garnish, and serve piping hot.

SOURCE: ANON

Note: This recipe is similar to Welsh Rabbit

Snickerdoodles
Also known as 'Sneaky Doodles'

2 3/4 cups plain flour
2 teaspoons cream of tartar
1 teaspoon baking soda
1/4 teaspoon salt
230 g butter, at room temperature
1 1/2 cups sugar
2 large eggs
1/4 cup extra sugar
2 tablespoons cinnamon

Place one rack in the top third and one rack in bottom third of oven, and preheat to 200° C (400°F). Line baking biscuit trays with baking paper. Sift together flour, cream of tartar, baking soda, and salt.

In the bowl of an electric mixer, combine butter and 1 1/2 cups sugar. Beat on medium speed until creamy and light - this takes a minute or two.

Add eggs, and beat until all ingredients are completely blended.

Add dry ingredients, except cinnamon, and beat well.

Cover the dough with plastic wrap and leave it to cool in the refrigerator for about an hour, to make it easier to handle.

Meanwhile mix together the extra 1/4 cup sugar and the ground cinnamon in a small bowl.

Use an ice cream scoop to cut balls out of the dough. Roll each ball in cinnamon and sugar mixture.

Put the balls about 5cm inches apart on the biscuit trays.

Bake for about five minutes then rotate the biscuit trays. Continue baking for another five minutes until the cookies are firm in the middle and small cracks appear. They will not go brown.

Take the trays out of the oven and leave them on a wire rack to cool for a few minutes before transferring the cookies to the rack. Store in an airtight container.

About Snickerdoodles

"A snickerdoodle is a type of cookie made with butter or oil, sugar, and flour rolled in cinnamon sugar. Eggs may also sometimes be used as an ingredient. Snickerdoodles are characterized by a cracked surface and can be crisp or soft depending on preference. Baked in an oven, these cookies are crispy on the outside and soft and gooey on the inside.

"Snickerdoodles are often referred to as "sugar cookies". However, traditional sugar cookies are often rolled in white sugar whereas snickerdoodles are rolled in a mixture of white sugar and cinnamon.

"Etymology

"The Joy of Cooking claims that snickerdoodles are probably German in origin, and that the name is a corruption of the German word Schneckennudeln (lit. "snail noodles"), a kind of pastry. A different author suggests that the word "snicker" comes from the German word Schnecke, which describes a snail shape. Yet another hypothesis suggests that the name has no particular meaning or purpose and is simply a whimsically named cookie that originated from a New England tradition of fanciful cookie names."

SOURCE: WIKIPEDIA

Everlasting Syllabub

1/4 pint (150 ml) White wine
2 Tbls Lemon juice
2 tsp. Lemon Zest (plus extra to decorate)
3oz (75 g) Caster Sugar
1/2 pint (300 ml) Double cream

Put the wine, lemon juice, zest, and sugar into a bowl. Leave for at least 3 hours. Add the cream and whip until the mixture stands in soft peaks. Transfer to 6 wine or sundae glasses and decorate with lemon zest. Chill for several hours before serving!

Brandy Everlasting Syllabub

1 lemon, zest and juice
3oz (75 g) Caster sugar
1-2 Tbls Brandy
2 Tbls Sweet Sherry
1/2 pint (300 ml) Double cream
Lemon Twists, to decorate

Soak the lemon zest in the juice for 2-3 hours, then mix with sugar, brandy, and sherry. Stir until dissolved. Whip the cream lightly, until it is just beginning to hold its shape, then gradually add the liquid, whipping continuously. Take care not to over-beat. Chill before serving in glasses, decorated with lemon twists!

Orange Everlasting Syllabub

Use 2 Tbls of an orange liqueur in place of the white wine or brandy/sherry mixture and the juice and zest of a medium orange in place of the lemon juice and zest. Reduce the sugar to 2oz. (50g). Allow to chill, then whip. Serve quickly, as this version separates into 2 layers when chilled.

SOURCE: CAMPBELL BURY, 1844

Syllabub I

570 ml/1 pint sherry or white wine
½ grated nutmeg
sugar to taste
900 ml/1½pt milk

Put the wine into a bowl, with the grated nutmeg and plenty of pounded sugar, and add it to the milk.

Clotted cream may be held on the top, with pounded cinnamon or nutmeg and sugar; and a little brandy may be added to the wine before the milk is put in.

In some countries, cider is substituted for the wine: when this is used, brandy must always be added.

Warm milk may be poured on from a spouted jug or teapot; but it must be held very high.

SOURCE: BEETON 1861

Syllabub II

Put one quart of milk in a double boiler, a pinch of salt, and one small stick of cinnamon. When hot, sweeten to taste and add the yolks of five eggs by dipping hot milk carefully on to the yolks.

Set back into the boiler until smooth.

When cool, flavour with vanilla.

Beat the whites of two eggs to a stiff froth, and stir into custard.

Fill ball glasses two-thirds full, and heap on top whipped cream slightly sweetened and flavoured with vanilla.

SOURCE: SUNDAY TIMES, PERTH, WA 1909

About Syllabub

"Syllabub (also sillabub, sillibub) is a traditional English dessert, popular from the sixteenth to the nineteenth century. It is usually made from rich milk or cream seasoned with sugar and lightly curdled with wine. Mrs Beeton (1861) gives two recipes. One author's recipe says to mix the other ingredients together in a large bowl, 'place the bowl under the cow, and milk it full.'

"The recipe can be traced back to the time of the Tudor Dynasty. In its early variations it was a drink made of new milk and cider, with the cows milked directly into an ale pot. A variation known as an Everlasting Syllabub allows for the cream to rise and thicken by letting it stand for several days."

SOURCE: WIKIPEDIA

INDEX

SNOW

BIBLIOGRAPHY

Books

Bathurst: Ration Book Recipes - Making Do. Pub. Bathurst Regional Council, NSW, date unknown.

Baxter, 1913: Housekeeper's Encyclopedia. By Lucia Millet Baxter, Boston and New York, Houghton Mifflin company, 1913

Beeton, 1861: Mrs Beeton's Book of Household Management. By Isabella Beeton. Published Originally By S. O. Beeton in 24 Monthly Parts, 1859-1861. First Published in a Bound Edition 1861

Berlin 1906: The Berlin Cook Book, compiled by the ladies of Berlin, Waterloo and friends elsewhere. 1906. Berlin. Ontario, Canada, The News Record Print Shop. (During the First World War, Berlin was renamed Kitchener. It is now the city of Kitchener/Waterloo)

Blackman, 1917: War-time Cookery - Practical Recipes Designed to Aid in the Conservation Movement. By Mrs Edith Blackman. Ypsilanti Press, Ypsilanti, Michigan USA 1917

Farmer, 1918: The Boston Cooking-School Cook Book. By Fannie Merritt Farmer (1857–1915) Rev. ed., with additional chapters on the cold pack method of canning, on the drying of fruits and vegetables, and on food values. Boston: Little, Brown, and Company, 1918

Farmer, 1921: A New Book of Cookery, by Fannie Merritt Farmer (1857–1915). Boston: Little, Brown, and Company, 1921

Campbell Bury, 1844: The Lady's Own Cookery Book and New Dinner-table Directory, In which Will be Found a Large Collection of Original Receipts ... Adapted to the Use of Persons Living in the Highest Style, as Well as Those of Moderate Fortune. By Lady Charlotte Campbell Bury, Published for Henry Colburn, London, 1844

Chicago 1930: Mrs. D. Morgan in The Chicago Daily News Cook Book, 1930

Corson, 1877: The Cooking Manual Of Practical Directions For Economical Every-day Cookery. By Juliet Corson, New York, Dodd, Mead & Co 1877

Eaton, 1823: The Cook and Housekeeper's Complete and Universal Dictionary: Including a System of Modern Cookery, in all Its Various Branches. By Mary Eaton. PRINTED AND PUBLISHED BY J. AND R. CHILDS 1823.

Goudiss, 1918: Foods That Will Win The War And How To Cook Them. C. Houston Goudiss and Alberta M. Goudiss, 1918

Harlan, 1875: Breakfast, Luncheon and Tea. By Marion Harland [Mary Virginia Terhune] 1875

Howson, 1881: Home cookery, by Mrs H. Howson, 1881
Published by Jackson brothers, printers, Philadelphia USA

Kirk, 1929: Tried Favourites Cookery Book With Household Hints and Other Useful Information. By Mrs.E. W. Kirk. Twelfth and Enlarged Edition. Edinburgh: J. B. Fairgrieve, 7 & 9 Cockburn Street, London: Horace Marshall & Son, 125 Fleet Street and Temple House, Temple Avenue, E.C. By Appointment to H.M. the King. 1929

Kleber, 1915: The Suffrage Cookbook. Compiled by L. O. Kleber. Fireship Press, 1915

Luck, 1915: The Belgian Cook-Book. Ed. Mrs. Brian Luck, E. P. Dutton, 1915

McKenzie Hill, 1909: Salads, Sandwiches and Chafing-Dish Dainties, With Fifty Illustrations of Original Dishes. By Janet McKenzie Hill, Editor of "The Boston Cooking-School Magazine" and Author of "Practical Cooking and Serving" NEW EDITION WITH ADDITIONAL RECIPES, Boston, Little, Brown, and Company 1909

McKenzie Hill, 1918: Economical War-time Cook Book: Wheatless Breads, Victory Breads and Rolls, How to Use Wheat Substitutes, How to Conserve Sugar, How to Save Fats, Salads, Canning, Etc., Etc. By Janet McKenzie Hill (1852-1933) George Sully & Company, New York 1918

Meyer, 1898: A Practical Dictionary of Cookery: 1200 tested recipes By Ethel Meyer. London, J. Murray 1898

Ministry of Food, London, 1942: 'Food Facts for the Kitchen Front', by The Ministry of Food, London. "Food Facts No 31" under "What do you put in your 'Carried Meal'?" (Recipes from this book were also published in newspapers during WWII)

Patten, 1985: We'll Eat Again: How the housewives on the Kitchen Front kept a hungry nation fed on nothing but rations. By Margaret Patten. Hamlyn; 1st edition 1985

Patten, 2004: Post-war Kitchen: Nostalgic Food and Facts from 1945-1954 by Margaret Patten. Hamlyn; New edition 2004

P.W.M.U., 1904: P.W.M.U.Cookbook. Presbyterian Women's Missionary Union, Australia, 1904

Walsh, 1859: The English Cookery Book, Uniting Good Style with Economy. Collected by A Committee of Ladies. ed. JH Walsh 1859

Willey, 1884: The Model Cookbook, Containing Over 1000 Thoroughly Tested Recipes. By Mrs Frances Willey, RH Lisk 1884

Newspapers

The Advertiser (Adelaide, South Australia: 1889 - 1931)

Advocate (Burnie, Tasmania: 1890 - 1954)

Albany Advertiser (Western Australia: 1897 - 1950)

The Argus (Melbourne, Victoria: 1848 - 1956)

Australian Town and Country Journal (NSW : 1870 - 1907)

The Australian Women's Weekly (1933 - 1982)

Barrier Miner (Broken Hill, New South Wales: 1888 - 1954)

The Brisbane Courier (Queensland: 1864 - 1933)

Brownsville Herald, Texas, USA, November 22, 1931

Burra Record (South Australia: 1878 - 1954)

Cairns Post (Queensland: 1909 - 1954)

The Charleville Times (Brisbane, Queensland: 1896 - 1954)

The Central Queensland Herald (Rockhampton, Queensland: 1930 - 1956)

The Cumberland Argus and Fruitgrowers Advocate, Parramatta, NSW, 1895

The Daily News (Perth, Western Australia: 1882 - 1950)

The Dubbo Liberal and Macquarie Advocate (NSW : 1892 - 1927) Saturday 23 February 1907
Evelyn Observer and Bourke East Record (Vic. : 1902 - 1917)Friday 11 April 1913

Examiner (Launceston, Tasmania: 1900 - 1954)

Kyabram Union (Victoria: 1886 - 1894)

Liverpool Herald (NSW : 1897 - 1907) Saturday 27 August 1904

Los Angeles Times, November 22, 1929. "Practical Recipes," BY Mrs. J. R., Alhambra California.

The Mail (Adelaide, SA : 1912 - 1954) Saturday 13 December 1941

Mirror (Perth, Western Australia: 1921 - 1956)

Morning Bulletin (Rockhampton, Queensland, Australia: 1878 - 1954)

The North Eastern Ensign (Benalla, VIC. : 1872 - 1938) Friday 9 April 1886

The North Queensland Register (Townsville, Qld. : 1892 - 1905) Wednesday 8 December 1897

Northern Times (Carnarvon, Western Australia: 1905 - 1952)

The Queenslander (Brisbane, Queensland: 1866 - 1939)

The Register (Adelaide, SA : 1901 - 1929) Tuesday 3 February 1925

Sunday Times (Perth, Western Australia: 1902 - 1954)

The Sydney Morning Herald (New South Wales: 1842 - 1954)

Townsville Daily Bulletin (Queensland: 1885 - 1954)

Van Nuys News, California, USA, October 27, 1932, "Katherine Parsons' Cooking Column"

The West Australian (Perth, WA : 1879 - 1954) Friday 30 July 1937

The Western Champion and General Advertiser for the Central-Western Districts (Barcaldine, Qld. : 1892 - 1922)

Western Mail (Perth, Western Australia: 1885 - 1954)

Wikipedia

Worker (Brisbane, Queensland: 1890 - 1955)

Other Sources

Anne Cheall, http://www.fightingthrough.co.uk

The Ministry of Food (UK), 1939-1945

'Learning Food Economy' The Outlook, December 13, 1916

WEIGHTS & MEASURES

Conversion of Household Measures

Liquids

1 drop	1/20 ml
1 teaspoon	5 ml
1 tablespoon	15 ml
1 cup	250 ml

Weights

2.20 pounds (avoirdupois)	1 kilogram (kg)
1 pound (avoirdupois)	453.6 grams (approx.500)
1 ounce (1/16 pound)	28.4 grams

Fluid Equivalents

1 fluid ounce (oz.)	29.57 ml (approx. 30)
1 pint (pt.) (16 fl. oz.)	473.2 ml (approx. 500)

1 pint, in the Imperial system	20 fluid ounces
1 quart (qt.)	946.4 ml (approx. 1000)
1 quart, in the Imperial system	40 fluid ounces
1 gallon (gal.)	3785.6 ml (approx. 4000)
1 gallon, in the Imperial system	160 fluid ounces

Metric System Weights and Measures

1 kilogram (kg)	1000 grams
1 milligram (mg)	0.001 gram
1 litre (l)	1000 ml
1 millilitre (ml)	0.001 l

Visit our Website & Online Bookshop

www.leavesofgoldpress.com

Have you seen the companion to this book?

MOCK TOAD-IN-THE-HOLE
AND
OTHER VINTAGE 'MOCK' DISHES

Including delicacies such as
Mock Caviar, Mock Sausages, Mock Oysters, Mock Apple Pie,
Mock Macaroons, Mock Strawberries and Cream, Mock Ice,
Mock Almonds, Mock Bananas, Mock Yorkshire Puddings, Mock
Raspberry Jam, Mock Maple Syrup and Mock Brains.

Get the matching pair at all good bookshops

END

Cookery Notes